T0357325

EXPERIENCE JESUS. REALLY.

Also by John Eldredge

EXPERIENCE JESUS. REALLY.

FINDING REFUGE, STRENGTH, AND WONDER THROUGH EVERYDAY ENCOUNTERS WITH GOD

JOHN ELDREDGE

NEW YORK TIMES BESTSELLING AUTHOR

NELSON BOOKS

An Imprint of Thomas Nelson

Published in Nashville, Tennessee, by Nelson Books, an imprint of Thomas Nelson. Nelson Books and Thomas Nelson are registered trademarks of HarperCollins Christian Publishing, Inc.

Published in association with Yates & Yates, www.yates2.com.

Thomas Nelson titles may be purchased in bulk for educational, business, fundraising, or sales promotional use. For information, please email SpecialMarkets@ThomasNelson.com.

Unless otherwise noted, Scripture quotations are taken from The Holy Bible, New International Version®, NIV®. Copyright © 1973, 1978, 1984, 2011 by Biblica, Inc.® Used by permission of Zondervan. All rights reserved worldwide. www.Zondervan.com. The "NIV" and "New International Version" are trademarks registered in the United States Patent and Trademark Office by Biblica, Inc.® Scripture quotations marked AMP are taken from the Amplified® Bible (AMP). Copyright © 2015 by The Lockman Foundation. Used by permission. www.lockman.org. Scripture quotations marked GNT are taken from the Good News Translation® in Today's English Version—Second Edition. Copyright © 1992 American Bible Society. Used by permission. All rights reserved. Scripture quotations marked KJV are taken from the King James Version. Public domain. Scripture quotations marked THE MESSAGE are taken from *THE MESSAGE*. Copyright © 1993, 2002, 2018 by Eugene H. Peterson. Used by permission of NavPress. All rights reserved. Represented by Tyndale House Publishers, Inc. Scripture quotations marked NASB are taken from the (NASB®) New American Standard Bible®. Copyright © 1960, 1971, 1977, 1995, 2020 by The Lockman Foundation. Used by permission. All rights reserved. www.lockman.org. Scripture quotations marked NLT are taken from the Holy Bible, New Living Translation. Copyright © 1996, 2004, 2015 by Tyndale House Foundation. Used by permission of Tyndale House Publishers, Inc., Carol Stream, Illinois 60188. All rights reserved. Scripture quotations marked NKJV are taken from the New King James Version®. Copyright © 1982 by Thomas Nelson. Used by permission. All rights reserved. Scripture quotations marked PHILLIPS are from *The New Testament in Modern English* by J. B. Phillips. Copyright © 1960, 1972 J. B. Phillips. Administered by the Archbishops' Council of the Church of England. Used by permission.

Any internet addresses, phone numbers, or company or product information printed in this book are offered as a resource and are not intended in any way to be or to imply an endorsement by Thomas Nelson, nor does Thomas Nelson vouch for the existence, content, or services of these sites, phone numbers, companies, or products beyond the life of this book.

ISBN 978-1-4002-5307-4 (ITPE)

Library of Congress Cataloging-in-Publication Data

Names: Eldredge, John, 1960- author.
Title: Experience Jesus--really : finding refuge, strength, and wonder through everyday encounters with God / John Eldredge.
Description: Nashville, Tennessee : Nelson Books, [2025] | Includes bibliographical references. | Summary: "New York Times bestselling author John Eldredge reveals the path of the "ordinary mystic," and invites readers into the refuge of experiencing deep, lasting, real communion with Jesus"-- Provided by publisher.
Identifiers: LCCN 2024042913 (print) | LCCN 2024042914 (ebook) | ISBN 9781400208654 (hardcover) | ISBN 9781400208722 (ebook)
Subjects: LCSH: Spiritual life--Christianity. | Christian life.
Classification: LCC BV4501.3 .E4255 2025 (print) | LCC BV4501.3 (ebook) | DDC 248.2/2--dc23/eng/20241115
LC record available at https://lccn.loc.gov/2024042913
LC ebook record available at https://lccn.loc.gov/2024042914

Printed in the United States of America

25 26 27 28 29 LBC 6 5 4 3 2

With love and gratitude to my fellowship of
"ordinary mystics" around the world.

Contents

CONTENTS

The devil fears a soul in union with God as he fears God himself.

SAINT JOHN OF THE CROSS

1.

Help My Unbelief!

Jesus said to him, "If you can believe, all
things are possible to him who believes."
Immediately the father of the child cried out and
said with tears, "Lord, I believe; help my unbelief!"

MARK 9:23–24 NKJV

Faith has always been a fragile thing in the human heart. Precious, lifesaving, but fragile, in the way a coral reef is fragile, or a fawn in the woods. It is something to be *protected*.

Your faith is the key that opens the door to access Jesus, and having found him, you gain access to his help *and* the riches of his entire Kingdom! Without that key we are adrift on a gray, endless sea. This is why faith is your most valuable possession, worth more than all the wealth you could possibly accumulate.

But do you really think much about protecting your faith?

I marvel at how something so powerful could at the same time be so fragile, so easily shaken. But I suppose love is like that too—it can be undercut with a single devastating sentence from someone you trusted. My concern is that our faculty of faith—the ability to trust and believe—has been secretly eroded by something most of us are completely unaware of. It has to do with the fact that we are, all of us, Disciples of the Internet.

If that seems unfair, if you repel the idea that you might be a Disciple of the Internet, consider this: You are a disciple of the system that tutors you, where you turn on a daily basis for guidance on living. For most people, that makes them Disciples of the Internet, even if they call themselves disciples of Christ. If you have a question, you go look it up—new developments for children with ADHD; how often normal married couples have sex; memory care for aging parents; the proper temperature to bake a potato. We do this all day, every day.

However, I'm not referring to whatever content it is you search for online. I'm talking about what we have learned from years of *the process itself.*

For one thing, the Internet has discipled your soul to expect immediate answers. You inquire and you are answered—immediately. Three million results in 0.003 seconds; there is no waiting. The saints of ages past would be aghast at that. Waiting was considered formational for the soul. They planted crops in the spring and harvested in the fall; there was no rushing things. If you wanted something from the market, you walked there and then you walked back, moving at a pace of about three miles an hour.

But now, when you turn to Jesus and you are not answered in the way the Internet answers, you feel he isn't listening or that you can't hear from him. You sadly believe the two of you are distant from one another, because your soul has been *programmed* for immediate responses. The notion of *lingering* before God doesn't fit with the pace we've come to expect.

That's one example, but the effects of Internet discipleship go far, far deeper.

Weary, Skeptical Pragmatism

To live just about anywhere on the planet is to have access to the entire base of human knowledge in a few clicks. (Our spiritual forebears would have been *aghast* at that too; they would have seen it as a seductive, malevolent trap for the soul. In fact, they probably would have concluded that The End had indeed come.)[i] So much information is available to us, on every conceivable subject, that we haven't noticed what it's done to us.

Someone forwards a video featuring a "leading neuroscientist" on the importance of vitamin B12 ("Everyone should be taking B12 for energy and mental health!"). We read a notable economist telling us that bonds are the safest place for our savings right now. We watch a TikTok video showing the correct way to exercise or lose weight. *Okay, we got this; we can thrive.*

But the very next day, everything we thought was reliable is overturned by new information.

Another expert steps forward to inform us, "Your anxiety might actually be *caused* by the amount of B12 you are taking; those levels are neurotoxic." "Bonds are a terrible decision right now." "The way you are exercising is damaging your body. Your weight-loss program has actually programmed your cells to *retain* weight." The leading cancer centers recommend you wear a hat and sunscreen to prevent skin cancer. Oops . . . new research shows that Americans now have a vitamin D *deficiency* because they wear hats and sunblock.

---

i. In 1982, the philosopher Buckminster Fuller observed the effect of accelerating change on human knowledge. In his model, all human knowledge—from architectural techniques to agriculture to animal husbandry—could be represented as a single unit in AD 1. From that time, it took 1,500 years for all knowledge to double. Then it doubled again in 250 years. Then again in 150. Depending on which Google strategist you read, human knowledge is now doubling in years or even months.

On and on, ad infinitum.

We cling to the belief that practical information is the way to salvation. But information is continually contradicted, undermined, laid waste—leaving us feeling fragile, vulnerable, and cynical. It's like we've been caught within some sort of ancient Eastern quandary parable:

A woman whose child was dying came before the gods to seek their help.

"Please save my child," she prayed.

The gods responded by putting three boxes before her.

"In one of these boxes is the cure to save your child's life."

"The second will release famine in the land. The third will bring a curse on someone you do not know."

"Choose as best you can, or choose not to choose at all."

Information feels like our salvation, but information is seductive and capricious, friends; it offers refuge, then takes it away the very next moment.

Life with the Internet has severely eroded our confidence that we can even know what's true *while accelerating the drive to get to the truth.* Like a gambling addiction. We want to thrive; we want our loved ones to thrive. We're convinced that in order to thrive, we must find the right information, "the latest science." But that information keeps changing, the truths we hold today overturned by new information tomorrow.

This whiplash has made skeptics of us all—weary skeptics.

The cinnamon you use has lead in it. This renowned car company is found guilty of installing illegal devices to bypass emissions tests on their vehicles. Russian hackers generate fake news to influence global elections. That photo you loved that a friend posted? It was fake, AI generated.

Do you see what I mean, folks?

The Internet has eroded your capacity to *believe* through constant contradiction and exposures of deceit. We lose confidence in our capacity to *trust*; our faculty of faith collapses into suspicion.

How confident are you right now that you can get to the real news—the truth, the whole truth, and nothing but the truth? How confident are you that your financial future is being well guarded by the folks in charge of guarding it? How confident are you that your government is telling you the truth?

Long-term suspicion can lead to what one paper called "active, sophisticated attributional thinking," meaning we begin to infer ulterior motives in others that may not in fact be there, but that nevertheless diminish our ability to believe.[1] (Think politics—how "the other guys" are always up to no good.) The Internet has discipled us into weary, skeptical pragmatists.

You would think we could keep this limited to exercise and politics, but it has bled into our ability to access God.

Can We Really Experience Jesus?

The Internet has taught its disciples that there shall be no mystery to anything. We can get to the bottom of any question, lay open the bare facts to any secret. In fact, if there *is* mystery, we've been thoroughly discipled to question it. Mystery equals some probable deception or scandal. Facts are safe; nothing else is.

The eradication of mystery would also be shocking to our spiritual forebears. We feel that in order to experience Jesus and access his help, we need to understand the spiritual like we do nutrition, exercise, or retirement plans. A friend asked me this week, "Yes, but how do I love God? How do I take refuge in him? I mean, *practically* speaking?"

It is the question of the person discipled by the Internet.

As soon as you hear the demand for the practical, in simple, clear immediate steps, you know you are talking to a Disciple of the Internet. It is a very different question, a different posture than someone approaching a saint of ages past and asking, "Teach me to commune with God."

If I told you, "The Bible says that prayer is powerful," you would say, "Sure." If I told you, "I saw this study on how prayer rewired the brains of older nuns into a more peaceful frame of mind," you would say, "Wow. That is so cool. I think I want to pray more."

It's madness, this addiction. My friend was asking *how* in the same way he would ask, "How do I change the water filter in my refrigerator?" His question (I know him well) was filled with demand for the mechanics, as in, *Make God like my refrigerator—not mysterious, but concrete.* Give me the practical. Make it practical. Give me the latest science or I won't believe you; in fact, I hardly believe you now.

Do you understand that to make Jesus and his Kingdom practical is to strip it of all wonder, mystery, and *power*?

It's like asking for the mechanics of falling in love, enjoying sunlight on the ocean, comforting a frightened child. It's like refusing to trust laughter until someone explains the neuroscience. Honestly, asking, "How do I love God?" is like asking, "How do I love my son, my daughter?" The heart knows how to love without being told the latest research, for heaven's sake.

This is the bind we've been discipled into—our weary, skeptical pragmatism keeps us from experiencing the God we are dying without.

And there is a way out.

Thank God, there is a way out of the madness and into the joys of daily, rich experiences of Jesus. God and his beautiful Kingdom are much more accessible than your cultural moment has conditioned you to believe and *experience*.

This is very, very good news.

The Fresh Air of the Mystics

There is a tradition within Christendom that can help us out of the terrible bind we're in as Disciples of the Internet (not to mention every other fatiguing thing this age has done to us). A beautiful, historic fellowship within the Christian story of men and women called (by others) Christian mystics. I'm guessing you might recognize names like Augustine, Francis of Assisi, Thomas Aquinas, Brother Lawrence, Julian of Norwich, Martin Luther, Teresa of Avila, John of the Cross.[ii]

Many of the desert fathers and mothers would have been called mystics. So, too, would most of the Irish monks (men and women) that spread across that once-wild island seeking hermitages in the wilderness, which spread into little monastic communities and then leapt across the sea and evangelized Europe.

Once upon a time, the label "mystic" was intended as a term of respect or reverence, as in "saint" or, better still, "true follower of Jesus who has regular experiences with God."

---

ii. Yes, Aquinas and Luther. See Robert Barron, *Thomas Aquinas, Spiritual Master* (Word on Fire Academic, 2022), 1; Bengt Hoffman, *Luther and the Mystics* (Augsburg, 1976), 190.

But for us, living in the ashes of the Enlightenment, the word "mystic" has been hijacked to mean either "someone slightly crazy and out of touch with reality" or someone practicing a sort of pagan spirituality. There are oddballs, of course, in every movement. But as soon as we read the Christian mystics' writings and learn something of their lives, we discover that they were actually ordinary men and women who were *the most in touch with reality*; they experienced Jesus and the beauty of his Kingdom.

Bishops and cardinals came to the humble Carmelite friar Brother Lawrence for counsel and discipleship because this simple man had such a sweet communion with Jesus. He wrote,

> There is not in the world a kind of life more sweet and delightful, than that of a continual conversation with God; those only can comprehend it who practice and experience it.[2]

There was nothing strange or heretical about it; Brother Lawrence was a normal Christian. As Chesterton explained,

> Mysticism keeps men sane. As long as you have mystery you have health; when you destroy mystery you create morbidity. The ordinary man has always been sane because the ordinary man has always been a mystic. He has permitted the twilight. He has always had one foot in earth and the other in fairyland.[3]

Chesterton, a devout Christian, meant by "fairyland" the world of wonder and mystery children accept as real, and which Christians understand to be the beautiful unseen realm, the rest of the Kingdom of God. One foot on earth and one in the realm the Scriptures call "the heavens," which is no less real.

Friends—we need daily encounters with Jesus; that is what we are after. Nothing else will address the human condition. The apostle Paul did not come to Christ because someone showed him the latest research. He had an undeniable, personal encounter with Jesus on the Damascus Road, which not only transformed his faith but the future of Christianity. Paul went on to have many encounters with Jesus, which would make him one of the early mystics. And when the apostle John—also a mystic in the truest sense of the word—wrote to his disciples about the true nature of life with Christ, he said this:

> **WE NEED DAILY ENCOUNTERS WITH JESUS; THAT IS WHAT WE ARE AFTER.**

> From the very first day, we were there, taking it all in—we heard it with our own ears, saw it with our own eyes, verified it with our own hands. The Word of Life appeared right before our eyes; we saw it happen! And now we're telling you in most sober prose that what we witnessed was, incredibly, this: The infinite Life of God himself took shape before us.
>
> We saw it, we heard it, and now we're telling you so you can experience it along with us, this experience of communion with the Father and his Son, Jesus Christ. Our motive for writing is simply this: We want you to enjoy this, too. (1 John 1:1–4 THE MESSAGE)

Biblical Christianity was always, *always* meant to be deeply experiential. There are thousands of Muslims coming to faith in Christ right now through actual encounters with Jesus in dreams and visions.[4] These undeniable encounters secure their faith against the immediate persecution they often experience.

Tragically, too many Christians have lost the experience of God in this hour, due in no small part to their discipleship to the Internet and everything else this age has done to the human soul. Recovering the daily experience of Jesus is indispensable to recovering and securing faith in this hour. So let me quote Brother Lawrence again: "There is not in the world a kind of life more sweet and delightful, than that of a continual conversation with God; those only can comprehend it who practice and experience it."

Now, I realize I'm taking an enormous risk talking about "mystics." But there are times when great risks must be taken, and this crisis we are in certainly qualifies. We will unpack the word "mystic" and its embodiment in the pages to come. If you limit yourself to things you already understand and experience, there won't be much reason to read a book, travel, read the news, or walk in the woods, will there? Thankfully, these humble, holy men and women generously wrote about their experiences and invited others to experience Jesus and his Kingdom as the normal Christian life. In truth, the "mystical" element of our forefathers and mothers is much, much broader than we've been led to believe.

I have interacted with thousands of men and women around the globe whom I would call "ordinary mystics": normal folks living out their lives in normal occupations but saturated with a rich sense of God's presence and daily experiences with Jesus. Many have become dear friends. I want to invite you to recover this life. It is, as the apostle John pointed out, the one God always intended you to have.

And it will prove an absolute rescue to your faith.

PAUSE

Weary Disciple of the Internet, your soul has also been conditioned to take in massive amounts of content every day—far beyond the soul's ability to absorb. You think it's normal, but it is not.

Precious truths are washed away every hour by waves of incoming content. It's like pouring water into a glass already filled with good wine; it dilutes and dilutes while it spills over the sides and onto the floor.

So pause.

Take a few deep breaths.

———o———

We are going to take a soul's pace through this book.

Reflect before you move on. I said some pretty important things in chapter 1. It should have stopped you in your tracks.

Linger with it a moment.

2.

What Children and Mystics Know

The Christian of the future will be a
mystic or . . . will not exist at all.

KARL RAHNER

Repeated processes shape the soul; this has been core to discipleship for millennia.

It was inevitable that years of Internet life would shape our souls whether we wanted it to or not. As a friend said, "It's not that we've done something wrong; something wrong has been done to us."

Discipleship to the Internet has shaped your soul to expect immediate answers to your questions; given you a deep suspicion to all forms of mystery; fueled your addiction that the "practical" is the real stuff of life; while eroding your confidence that you can know anything for certain because yesterday's facts are savagely overturned. We are all worn out from this way of operating in the world because *there is no life in it*.

There is no life in it.

No wonder people have a hard time experiencing Jesus.

If you tell a child, "We're going to the beach tomorrow!" their immediate response is not, "Yeah . . . maybe. We'll see. Did you even check the weather?" That's the adult response. "Maybe we shouldn't—did you see online that there is a sewage issue on the coast this year?" A child simply receives the promise of adventure, and they will have the joy of both a day full of anticipation of going to the beach as well as going to the beach itself! Double the joy! Because children don't operate from a posture of weary skepticism, cynicism, and "I'll believe it when you show me the science."

Maybe remembering this will help us grasp what Jesus was trying to address when he said, "Truly I tell you, unless you change and become like little children, you will never enter the kingdom of heaven" (Matthew 18:3).

Never enter are pretty strong words. Never?

Jesus often acts like a firefighter rescuing victims trapped in a burning building. He says extremely serious things because the situation is extremely serious.

Here he is trying to rescue us from the barrier to experiencing God and his Kingdom that has been formed *within* us by the time we reach adulthood— the weary, skeptical cynicism . . . the *guardedness*. Jesus says, "I have so much to show you, so much to offer you. But you're going to have to let go the cynicism, skepticism, and pragmatism. Open yourself up to belief again. Simply trust, like a child does."

JESUS OFTEN ACTS LIKE A FIREFIGHTER RESCUING VICTIMS TRAPPED IN A BURNING BUILDING. HE SAYS EXTREMELY SERIOUS THINGS BECAUSE THE SITUATION IS EXTREMELY SERIOUS.

You can do this, friends; you really can.

You can surrender all that discipleship to the Internet has done to you. I choose the word *surrender* because we cling to our skepticism for self-protection. Jesus seems to think that it's actually not that difficult to allow fresh confidence to infuse your capacity to believe; he knows the child-heart is still in there.

Our rescue lies in this: The mystics knew that you don't need the latest science in order to believe; you don't have to understand something in order to experience it. They saw mystery as a *good* thing, part of the joy of discovering God and his glorious Kingdom. They knew nothing of how sunlight on our skin produces vitamin D in our cells (do *you* really?). But they bared their skin to the sun anyways and rejoiced in God for his goodness. So Patrick prayed,

> I arise today
> Through the strength of heaven:
> Light of sun,
> Radiance of moon,
> Splendor of fire.[1]

And a thousand years later Saint Francis sang,

> Be praised, my Lord, through all your creatures,
> especially Sir Brother Sun,
> who brings the day; and you give light through him.
> And he is beautiful and radiant in all his splendour!
> Of you, Most High, he bears the likeness.[2]

There is something wonderfully childlike about this; they have one foot in nature and the other in the unseen part of God's great

Kingdom. They understood in their hearts that we can open ourselves to the presence of God like we turn to enjoy the warmth of the sun. "Hearts unfold like flowers before thee, opening to the sun above," as Henry van Dyke wrote in a lovely, poetic phrase.[3] You don't have any of the severe rationalism here that has crept into parts of Christendom; you don't find the "prove it to me" attitude so pervasive among Disciples of the Internet. Which is why these saints were able to have such profound

> THE MYSTICS KNEW THAT YOU DON'T NEED THE LATEST SCIENCE IN ORDER TO BELIEVE; YOU DON'T HAVE TO UNDERSTAND SOMETHING IN ORDER TO EXPERIENCE IT.

encounters with Jesus and his Kingdom, producing a resilience in them we are famished to know for ourselves.

Don't Freak Out

I realize the words "mystic" and "mysticism" carry some baggage, but we needn't be afraid. These are good words and need to be reclaimed by the Christian community. There is holy mysticism and unholy mysticism, just as there is holy and unholy sex, art, science, and just about anything else. Sure—there have been mystics who were heretics down through the ages; in this hour many people are seeking "transcendent experiences" through rituals like meditation retreats and ceremonies using ayahuasca. Those things open you to the spiritual realm all right, but the kingdom of darkness is what rushes in. We will stick to the holy tradition of biblical, *Christian* mysticism, which again is simply the regular experience of the one true God as revealed in Jesus Christ and his vast, beautiful Kingdom.[i]

If you look through the biblical narrative in the Scriptures and read the saints down through the ages, it is impossible to miss the invitation—we are *all* meant to experience God and the beauty of his Kingdom in deep and profound ways. There is no other way home. There is no other life that is life itself. In this light, as I pointed out earlier, the apostle John was a mystic, as was Saint Paul. David was a mystic; certainly Adam and Eve were.

Which makes Jesus of Nazareth the greatest mystic of all, for his life was unbroken communion with God his Father, and his experiences are *windows* into what it is like to live in God's full Kingdom.

When we understand mysticism as simply *the daily experience of God and his Kingdom*, we can say that mysticism is the normal Christian life. Which is to say, it is human existence put back on track. This is what Eve and Adam enjoyed, and it is central to God's restoration of humanity.

Ordinary Mystics

Evelyn Underhill was a deep lover of Jesus from the turn of the last century, and she wrote one of the definitive studies on the Christian mystics. Evelyn earnestly wanted people to understand that mysticism is completely normal; every person has a latent capacity to experience God. You were created for this very thing, so the faculty lies deep within your being.[4]

---

i.   If you haven't yet noticed, a number of prominent Christian authors are saying the same thing, from Catholic Bishop Robert Barron to Orthodox writer Rod Dreher and Protestants John Mark Comer and Jamie Smith.

Prior to the Age of Reason and its monstrous offspring the Internet, we wouldn't even have to use the word "mystic" at all. These are just normal Christians, friends of God. If it helps, you can substitute the word "amphibian," as in someone who lives comfortably in two worlds, both the spiritual realm and the physical. When you pray, for example, you are standing (perhaps kneeling) somewhere here on terra firma, planet earth—but you are *communing* with the unseen realm above. Heaven and earth meet when you pray. In a very "mystical" sort of statement, Paul writes that in God "we live and move and have our being" (Acts 17:28). We are surrounded with the presence of God. We swim in it every day, which fits the "amphibious" idea of human nature and experience. The joy comes when we learn to tune in to it, give our attention to his presence, drinking deeply from it.

There is so much more Scripture has to say about the "amphibious life" of Christians; it's right there on nearly every page. Hebrews says that when we pray we can "come boldly to the throne of grace"[5]—an invitation to practice our amphibious nature by *intentionally* coming into the presence of God (I'll say more about all of this as we go on). Further, we are assured that Christ now lives within us, which means that we can also experience his presence deep within our own being. So when the fifteenth-century mystic Thomas à Kempis offers the following invitation, he is speaking of an experience that is completely accessible to every human being:

> WE ARE ASSURED THAT CHRIST NOW LIVES WITHIN US, WHICH MEANS THAT WE CAN ALSO EXPERIENCE HIS PRESENCE DEEP WITHIN OUR OWN BEING.

Turn to God with all your heart, and you will see the kingdom of God come unto you. .... Christ will come to you offering His consolation, if you prepare a fit dwelling for Him in your heart. His visits with the inward man are frequent, His communion sweet and full of consolation, His peace great, and His intimacy wonderful indeed.[6]

This sweet, healing communion is something the people of God, from every tradition, have written about down through the centuries. It's all quite natural, really, and wonderful. We get the joys of coffee, bicycles, and sunsets, *and* the presence of the Living God, together with the unseen riches of his great Kingdom! That's why I prefer the term "ordinary mystics" to remind us that this is not something exceptional or rare. It might be *unfamiliar*, but so are the California redwoods if you've never walked among those fairy-tale forests. So is the immense serenity of the Sahara Desert. But unfamiliar does not mean something is *unreal*. Communion with Christ is completely real and accessible, and it's filled with more wonder than the redwoods and the Sahara.

> COMMUNION WITH CHRIST IS COMPLETELY REAL AND ACCESSIBLE, AND IT'S FILLED WITH MORE WONDER THAN THE REDWOODS AND THE SAHARA.

To ensure we don't get hung up over the use of the word "mystic," let's clarify Christian mysticism. Granted, the writings of some of the famous mystics are so ethereal that they add to the perception that mysticism involves wild visions and ecstasies.

But it is not so.

The ordinary mystic, the friend of Jesus . . .

- Enjoys the palpable presence of Jesus, their Papa, and the Holy Spirit.[ii]
- Hears the voice of God in daily living.
- Is able to enter into an inner communion with Jesus, who dwells in their heart.
- Draws their life from God.
- Is not surprised by things like miracles breaking into everyday life.

Turning for Home

Humanity at this moment is living in utter poverty. Nearly all of the wonder, beauty, and enchantment of this world and the God who made it has been thoroughly stripped away and deconstructed, leaving us nowhere to take refuge in the storms of life. The cynical pursuit of the pragmatic prevents us from experiencing life in the shelter of God.

But there is a way home. The Kingdom of God hasn't lessened one bit, even though mankind has dismissed it. There is profound refuge and healing to be found in Jesus and in his Kingdom; it surrounds us all the time. The ordinary mystic says, "All these things are real. I do not need to understand, but I do anticipate experiencing them as I learn the ways of God and his Kingdom."

It would be good to have a safe place to come home to.

---

ii. I'm intentionally using the word "Papa" instead of "Heavenly Father" for two reasons: (1) Scripture does, when it teaches us to call out "Abba" (Romans 8:15), and (2) because highly religious phrases like "our Heavenly Father" make him seem remote and unapproachable, the very thing he wiped away forever in the coming of Jesus.

It would be good to have a safe place you could go to anytime you need.

And it would be wonderful indeed if you could tap into all of the extraordinary beauty and provision of God's Kingdom anytime you needed. It would be so marvelous it would almost be like stumbling into a fairy tale that was utterly true.

You can.

You must.

Shall we venture on?

PAUSE

Take a few deep breaths.

Linger and reflect.

Perhaps this prayer is timely:

O Jesus, heal this effect that the world has had upon me. Heal the ravages of discipleship to the Internet. I surrender my skepticism, my cynicism, my "prove it to me" attitude. I surrender my unbelief. Heal the faculty of faith in me. I want to live with childlike trust in you and in our Papa. I want to recover wonder and anticipation. I want to experience the Kingdom of God each and every day. Jesus, I surrender cynicism, skepticism, and the practical. Breathe new life into faith in me.

3.

Gimme Shelter

Where should we go? No place is safe.

A MOTHER IN THE MIDDLE EAST, MARCH 2024

In the dawn of our childhood, we lived with God in a garden paradise. We walked with our Abba Father in the cool of the day, in conversational intimacy. We were ordinary mystics, drinking in the rich company of God and the fullness of his Kingdom. Eden was our home; we flourished in the shelter of a paradise where heaven and earth met.[i]

But we lost that home, and we have been seeking refuge ever since.

There are many riches, wonders, and adventures to be had as an ordinary mystic, a friend of Jesus, living in partnership with him in this hour. But I think we need to begin by getting into a safe place. We are meant to live within the refuge of God. Humans wandering outside

---

i. The garden of Eden is believed to have been at the top of a mountain. In the ancient worldview, this is where God's realm (the heavens) and earth meet. Thus the garden was the temple of the Lord. Humanity, first in Adam and Eve, was meant to live in that marriage of realms very comfortably. Michael Heiser, *Unseen Realm: Recovering the Supernatural Worldview of the Bible* (Lexham, 2015), 47.

that refuge, even Christians, are dying from soul starvation and exposure in every way.

Let's begin our recovery from Internet discipleship by seeking first the refuge of our souls in the presence of God. Every human being is created to live and move through this world as an ordinary mystic. We can learn to use our amphibious nature to get back into the refuge of God.

> EVERY HUMAN BEING IS CREATED TO LIVE AND MOVE THROUGH THIS WORLD AS AN ORDINARY MYSTIC.

Life Outside of Eden

Every time I wander the British Isles, particularly on Scotland's and Ireland's rugged coastlines, I'm drawn to the remains of ancient stone towers—some of them thousands of years old. Covered with moss and lichen, partly broken down, they fascinate me; I walk around them, climb into them if I can. Most are on the wild and windswept coastlines or even more remote outer islands. People living in those exposed places built these places of refuge against seaborne raiders, slave traders, and invaders.

Later came the famous round towers of Ireland that dot the countryside wherever a monastic village once flourished. In the American Southwest we have the Anasazi cliff dwellings, beautiful stone villages built into caves and ledges halfway up gigantic rock faces. When the ladder was pulled up, there was no way to access the community from above or below.

These are monuments to refuge—the human need for refuge.

It is an ancient and primal need, always there in the back of our consciousness. It is a need given to us by our Creator, and it breaks to the surface in times of uncertainty. And as any historian will tell you, those times mark human history far more than the settled and secure times do. Notice how often the mystics who wrote the psalms talk about refuge:

> But let all who take refuge in you be glad;
>> let them ever sing for joy.
> Spread your protection over them,
>> that those who love your name may rejoice in
>>> you. (Psalm 5:11)

> The LORD is my rock, my fortress and my deliverer;
>> my God is my rock, in whom I take refuge . . . my
>>> stronghold. (Psalm 18:2)

> Hear my cry, O God;
>> listen to my prayer.
> From the ends of the earth I call to you,
>> I call as my heart grows faint;
>> lead me to the rock that is higher than I.
> For you have been my refuge,
>> a strong tower against the foe. (Psalm 61:1–3)

And of course the famous Psalm 91:

> Whoever dwells in the shelter of the Most High
>> will rest in the shadow of the Almighty.
> I will say of the LORD, "He is my refuge and my fortress,
>> my God, in whom I trust."
> Surely he will save you. (verses 1–3)

They are reporting an actual *experience* of safety and well-being in the presence of God.

And remember—at the time of their writing, the people dwelling in the Middle East lived in constant uncertainty; one never knew when raiding nomads or the armies of mighty, savage nations might appear on the horizon, sweeping through with devastation in their wake. Israel sat along the crossroads of ancient trade routes; armies used those routes to move swiftly north and south. Racial hatred and violence were the norm. Safe places were extremely important, like the fortress at Tell el-'Umeiri, a city with a moat sixteen feet deep, an outer wall sixteen feet high, and the city wall made of two layers filled with earth to withstand battering rams.[1]

These folks took refuge very seriously.

The developed world with all its comforts, resources, and technologies has lulled us into thinking that our safety is found in where we live, in public services, in our medical coverage and retirement plans. But we're especially convinced that *knowing the right facts and techniques will secure our lives,* so we scramble to make sure we have the latest science, the irrefutable data—only to have them overturned the next day. This double bind has made skeptics of us all—increasingly anxious skeptics.

I'm watching the climbing rates of anxiety among children and adults, and as a therapist this all seems to be a "tip of the iceberg" piece of data. (Here we go—I have to use the latest research in order to convince you of my concern.)

In the last thirty years anxiety disorders have risen 50 percent among adults. Currently, 45.3 percent of young adults have symptoms of an anxiety disorder. Nearly one in every two young people? These are folks living in the unprecedented safety and comfort of

America; what would the data be in places around the world experiencing civil war, earthquakes, political collapse?

Humanity is feeling the intensity of the hour and the need for a true place of emotional, mental, and spiritual refuge.

And no wonder. There are hundreds of millions of forcibly displaced people in the world and even higher numbers of migrants. War, poverty, persecution, and fear have huge masses of humanity on the move; a huge exodus is taking place as people leave rural areas for work in global cities.[2] All these numbers are at all-time highs, and they don't account for *internal* displacement like homelessness, poverty, or the impact of natural disasters. (Natural disasters in the US displaced 2.5 million people in 2023 alone.[3])

The world is reeling from chaos and catastrophe. Where is home? Where can we offer refuge to others?

You've seen the gripping photos of the life jackets piled up on the beaches of Greece. People digging with their bare hands for victims of earthquakes around the world. The tent cities in places like Gaza. This morning I looked at photos of one refugee camp harboring *over a million people* in tents, with children wandering empty streets looking for food. Even if these things aren't currently taking place where you live—though natural disasters have swept the globe—watching repeated news reports about them is deeply upsetting.

Trauma and Refuge

The anxiety iceberg and a host of other data lead me to believe that humanity is operating in a collective state of trauma, ranging from a low-grade fever for some to extreme debilitation in others—the anxieties of a teenager questioning their gender identity to the refugees fleeing war-torn regions on foot, carrying their only belongings in plastic bags. Some state or experience of trauma seems to be shared by nearly everyone on the planet.

I was reading a story recently from the great age of polar exploration at the turn of the nineteenth century, when men with nothing close to modern equipment raced to the poles for science, personal honor, and glory. The stories of the life-and-death role that *shelter* played are simply gripping. In this particular tale, a group of men had gone out from the refuge of base camp in temperatures never before experienced. They journeyed seventy miles on foot, pulling heavy sledges with all their gear through snow and ice.

> We had spent days in reaching this place through the darkness in cold such as had never been experienced by human beings. We had been out for four weeks under conditions in which no man had existed previously for more than a few days, if that. During this time we had seldom slept except from sheer physical exhaustion . . . and every minute of it we had been fighting for the bed-rock necessaries of bare existence, and always in the dark.[4]

It is a parable for me of human experience.

At their farthest point from base camp, the weather began to collapse. The men built a shelter, something between a stone hut and an igloo with a canvas roof. Then a hurricane fell on them.

> The roof of our igloo was being wrenched upwards and then dropped back with great crashes . . . everything was six or eight inches under snow. . . . The tension became well-nigh unendurable: the waiting in all that welter of noise was maddening.[5]

And then it went.

The top of the door opened in little slits and that green Willesden canvas flapped into hundreds of little fragments and fewer seconds than it takes to read this. The uproar of it all was indescribable. Even above the savage thunder of that great wind on the mountain came the lash of the canvas as it was whipped to tiny little strips. The highest rocks which we had built into our walls fell upon us, and a sheet of drift came in.[6]

Honestly, when I look at the world, when I see the battle raging for the destruction of the human race in the unseen realm, this does not seem far from our present situation.

The good news is, against unspeakable odds those men made it home. They made it home.

If the Gospel is gospel at all, it must have something to offer besieged humanity in terms of refuge. *Experiential* refuge, which is something the mystics knew about.

I believe ordinary mysticism holds the key, both for refuge and the healing of trauma.

> I BELIEVE ORDINARY MYSTICISM HOLDS THE KEY, BOTH FOR REFUGE AND THE HEALING OF TRAUMA.

Unless You Become as Little Children

When our boys were young, they would gather blankets, pillows, and cushions in the basement and build elaborate forts. This was their most-played game, a weekly if not daily affair. Once constructed and made secure, blankets tucked into sofas, cushions piled up as barriers, they would take refuge inside. Sometimes to read by flashlight or share candy treasures, other times for imaginary games. But mostly just to tuck in and "be," to enjoy the experience itself.

You probably built forts as a child. A refrigerator box was an absolute gold mine of a discovery, for with a few windows cut out and some duct tape on the doors it was an instant fortress.

The building of forts is a universal childhood practice that researchers have become intrigued by. Carol Stock Kranowitz, author of *The Out-of-Sync-Child*, explains, "Forts help children reset their stressed bodies and brains. The darkness inside a fort eliminates the stimulus they do not need and intensifies what they do need . . . physical comfort and solitude . . . safety and control. We seek out comfort. We need to restore order."[7]

Simply put, it's a way of making their world smaller for a while.

And children are mystics by nature. They don't need to understand global weather patterns to find the evening snowfall utterly enchanting. They don't need to know the brain science behind their parents' love for them; they simply feel safe being loved. And yes— those forts aren't actually fortresses; they collapse rather easily. But the little mystic within experiences a level of comfort and assurance that I think most adults are famished for.

Everyone needs a place to feel safe.

Everyone needs somewhere to go to tuck in, where the world can feel small again or at least shut out for the time being.

It might be good to pause and reflect: What is your current safe place in the world? Where do you go for refuge—not only physically but emotionally, psychologically, spiritually?

We can be situated securely in Jesus Christ and in God our

Father, not merely as a symbol or metaphor but in actuality. As the French mystic Jeanne Guyon assures us,

> I have found it easy to obtain the presence of God. He desires to be more present to us than we desire to seek Him. He desires to give Himself to us far more readily than we desire to receive Him. . . . This is easier and more natural than breathing.[8]

Easier than breathing—wouldn't that be lovely? This experience of God's presence and refuge is entirely available to you. Friends, we live in times just as dangerous as those of our ancient forebears. Let us not be lulled into a false security by the material comforts around us. We must, we *must* learn the practice of Jesus as our refuge. And here is where it will prove helpful to allow yourself to become a mystic. If you can suspend your disappointment, skepticism, and fear for even a moment and allow your heart to turn toward Jesus, *run* toward him, you can experience refuge in him.

> *Jesus—I need refuge. Bring me into your refuge, Lord. Be my shield and strong tower. Be my safe place. I turn to you; I run to you. Be my refuge, Lord. Surround me with your presence and keep me.*
>
> *Holy Spirit, awaken my capacity to know and experience God. Awaken my ability to see and hear in the Kingdom of God. Make me an ordinary mystic.*

PAUSE

I hope you are moved to get on to the next chapters. But we are not going to blast through the book.

Pause

Breathe.

———o———

For every beautiful being God created, he has provided a habitat in which to flourish. Brook trout thrive happily in cold mountain streams. If you were to put them in the warm waters of the Caribbean, they would die. Stingrays, however, love that warm salt water; transfer them to a mountain stream and they will not survive a day.

Cloud forests cannot abide desert conditions. Coral reefs cannot tolerate freezing temperatures. The examples are nearly infinite—each beautiful creation has its perfect habitat.

We do too.

Human beings are meant to live within the safety of God, drawing our nourishment from our union with him. Not only believing in God but living *within* him.

We are also made to flourish in the fullness of God's Kingdom, part of which is this world we see—coffee with friends, bike rides, a good book. Part we cannot see but is equally necessary—the refuge of the Almighty and the vast wonders of God's Kingdom.

Not only is the world we live in constantly pulling you out of the habitat for which you are made, it is conditioning your soul against finding your way home.

The life of the ordinary mystic will help you get back.

That's what we are after.

4.

The Refuge of God

No shelter can be imaged at all comparable
to the protection of Jehovah's own shadow.
The Almighty himself is where his shadow
is, and hence those who dwell in his
secret place are shielded by himself.

CHARLES SPURGEON

That is a very mystical statement, by a Baptist minister no less, from the 1800s. It should make us curious.

Childlike curiosity will help you so much as we begin our practice of becoming ordinary Christian mystics by reflecting upon Psalm 91 (Spurgeon was speaking of Psalm 91). I suggest you read it once silently, then read it again out loud:

> Those who live in the shelter of the Most High
>   will find rest in the shadow of the Almighty.
> This I declare about the LORD:
> He alone is my refuge, my place of safety;
>   he is my God, and I trust him.

For he will rescue you from every trap

and protect you from deadly disease.

He will cover you with his feathers.

He will shelter you with his wings.

His faithful promises are your armor and protection.

Do not be afraid of the terrors of the night,

nor the arrow that flies in the day.

Do not dread the disease that stalks in darkness,

nor the disaster that strikes at midday.

Though a thousand fall at your side,

though ten thousand are dying around you,

these evils will not touch you.

Just open your eyes,

and see how the wicked are punished.

If you make the LORD your refuge,

if you make the Most High your shelter,

no evil will conquer you;

no plague will come near your home.

For he will order his angels

to protect you wherever you go.

They will hold you up with their hands

so you won't even hurt your foot on a stone.

You will trample upon lions and cobras;

you will crush fierce lions and serpents under

your feet!

The LORD says, "I will rescue those who love me.

I will protect those who trust in my name.

When they call on me, I will answer;

I will be with them in trouble.

I will rescue and honor them.

> I will reward them with a long life
> and give them my salvation." (NLT)

Notice your emotional reaction to the psalm—does it feel comforting, hopeful?

Or do you feel a twinge of hurt and suspicion, that old *Yeah* . . . *but* . . . ?

Ambivalence is not uncommon when we bring our human experiences to the Scriptures. That's okay; be gentle with the ambivalence as we seek a new experience of these promises. Set the skeptic aside for a moment; allow the mystic to come forth.

What exactly is being offered here?

How do we access it?

What was the experience of the mystics who wrote the psalms of refuge?

I will tip my hand—the refuge described here is not merely a state of mind, an assurance for the heart. It is an ontological *experience*—palpable, enjoyable, an encounter with God. Our being can actually take refuge within the being of God. We can experience being surrounded with the presence of God and his

> **IT IS AN ONTOLOGICAL EXPERIENCE— PALPABLE, ENJOYABLE, AN ENCOUNTER WITH GOD.**

mighty Kingdom in the same way we can jump into the ocean. Situated there, we can go on to experience many other realities of our God and his heavens.

Psalm 91 may have been written by Moses; some Jewish traditions believe so. The previous psalm (90) is attributed directly to Moses. Think of the conditions that Moses, his family, and his community were living under when they *experienced* in the fullest sense God as their refuge. They were slaves—the children, grandchildren, and great-grandchildren of slaves—wandering in a barren wilderness something like the surface of the moon for forty years. *Forty years.* They were hunted, constantly vigilant against nomadic raiders, having no clear vision yet of the Promised Land.

I would suggest it was somewhat traumatizing (living in constant uncertainty is traumatizing).

And yet Moses, a mystic who spoke with God face-to-face, "as a man speaks to his friend"[1] could say of God, "you have *always* been our home" (Psalm 90:1 GNT).

God is the home of every human soul. We are *from* him in every sense of the word. He thought of us before he created the world; he knit us together in our mother's womb; he breathed the Breath of Life into each one of us. All the days of our life were written in his book for us before one came to be. The mystery of this is exquisite, moving the poet William Blake to say,

> But trailing clouds of glory do we come
> From God, who is our home.[2]

This is key to embracing the reality ourselves, for if we *come* from God, then returning *to* him would be natural; we would be welcome there. We might even remember the way, in our heart of hearts. Can we forget the prodigal son, who though lost and dissolute could still turn for home? He knew in his heart it was still there.

The Most High, our Father, is the

THE MOST HIGH, OUR FATHER, IS THE ULTIMATE DWELLING PLACE. HERE WE DISCOVER TRUE COMFORT, SECURITY, AND REST.

ultimate dwelling place. Here we discover true comfort, security, and rest. But even more, he is the source of all healing of human trauma. He truly restores the soul as we take refuge in him.

There Is a Wild Dynamic Here

Let's come back to the ambivalence many people feel as they read the psalms of refuge, and especially these mighty promises God is making. How come this doesn't seem to be reliably true in human experience?

There is an honesty to Psalm 91 that you may have missed. With powerful images of refuge and fortress, we might misunderstand *the nature of the experience* if we don't grasp all the passages in the psalm.

There is war:

> . . . the arrow that flies by day . . .
> Though a thousand fall at your side,
>> though ten thousand are dying around you,
>> these evils will not touch you. (verses 5–7)

There is the need of angelic help:

> For he will order his angels
>> to protect you wherever you go. (verse 11)

There are demonic assaults (and victory over those assaults):

> You will trample upon lions and cobras;

you will crush fierce lions and serpents under
your feet! (verse 13)

And twice, the refuge of God is described in terms of rescue, or deliverance:

"I will rescue those who love me.
I will protect those who trust in my name.
When they call on me, I will answer;
I will be with them in trouble.
I will rescue and honor them." (verses 14–15)[3]

When we think about God as our strong tower, I think we assume something fixed and immovable, like a castle or those round towers in the British Isles. But war is savage and traumatizing, and this passage takes place in the midst of war. Demonic assault, I believe, is even more terrible; it is dark and overpowering in sinister ways. *Rescue* and *deliverance* are very different experiences than the static safety of a great fortress.

Perhaps our understanding of God as refuge needs to mature to accommodate something very active and dynamic. We will explore this more fully in the chapters ahead. But what I want you to grasp for this moment is that the refuge of God is not a static thing. Not one and done. You live in a story, friends, not a painting. It is played out in the harsh realities of a dangerous world. And *all* of the Kingdom of God is involved in our rescue.

Maybe, if we learn to find refuge in the midst of this wild and dangerous world, we can discover for ourselves what the mystics have known to be utterly and reliably true.

What Is the Secret Place?

In the New Testament, the author of the book of Hebrews makes an emphatic invitation: "So let us come boldly to the throne of our gracious God. There we will receive his mercy, and we will find grace to help us when we need it most" (Hebrews 4:16 NLT).

The ordinary saints and mystics down through the ages took this literally; I think it is meant to be taken literally. There is nothing figurative about it. Come boldly to the throne of God. The throne of God is an actual place; it is situated in the City of God in the heavens.[i] Have you read this as a literal invitation to an actual place? The mystics did and found themselves able to enter the heavens and come before God our Father.

We are invited to experience the rest of God's Kingdom, for we are sons and daughters of that Kingdom and it is our true home. This is essential to our recovery and resilience in an hour as rough as this one.

So, when the author of Psalm 91 invites us to take refuge in the shelter of the Most High, where does he have in mind? What actual place in the actual universe are we invited to?

The word for "shelter" in the opening verse ("Those who live in the shelter of the Most High") can be translated as a "hidden place" or "secret place"—the very experience children are searching for when building forts: "This is my secret, special place." A great deal has been written about the secret place of God by mystics through the ages, some of it exquisite and some of it so vague as to

---

i.   For the time being; then the City of God comes down as the New Jerusalem to the New Earth at the restoration of all things. Then Eden is restored, the mountain temple of our God bringing heaven and earth together as one. (The Tree of Life is there, proving Eden has returned.) See Revelation 21 and 22.

be unhelpful. If we are invited to take refuge in the secret place, it can't be so mysterious as to be beyond finding.

What is the inmost place of God? What is the absolute center?

His heart. Just as your heart is the very center of your being, so our Father's heart is the center of his.

As the twentieth-century mystic A. W. Tozer reminds us, "God is a Person, and in the deep of His mighty nature He thinks, wills, enjoys, feels, loves, desires and suffers as any other person may."[4]

> **WE ARE INVITED TO EXPERIENCE THE REST OF GOD'S KINGDOM, FOR WE ARE SONS AND DAUGHTERS OF THAT KINGDOM AND IT IS OUR TRUE HOME.**

The secret place of God is his heart, and we are invited to take refuge there! What privilege, what intimacy, what joy!

Trailing clouds of glory you came from the heart of God, and you can return to his heart. This is the truest and greatest homecoming of all. The presence of God—Father, Son, Holy Spirit—and the vast resources of his Kingdom are always nearby. But we do need to make conscious choices to take our refuge in God and his Kingdom. Otherwise we are taking refuge somewhere else.

(You might want to give some thought to where you look for safety these days—for a sense of well-being, centeredness, groundedness, and spiritual protection.)

Lord, I run to you right now. You are my refuge, my fortress, and I take refuge in you. I bring everything I am into you, Lord Jesus. Surround me with your protection; hide me deep in you.

Holy Spirit, help me into the refuge of God. Bring me into Papa's heart.

I think you will begin to see how important this is, and how wonderful.

I hope you continue to be moved to get to the next chapters. There are riches waiting in the pages ahead! But again, we are not going to blast through this book.

We are awash in Christian content, much of it excellent content—Bible podcasts, devotional apps, and of course your social threads. But content *about* Jesus is not the same as communion *with* Jesus. It's often a distraction.

So pause.

Breathe.

Let this seep down into your soul.

———o———

We had a home. It was in Eden. We dwelt in the garden temple of our God. It was our refuge. Eden was where the Living God, our Creator and Father, lived in rich communion with humanity.

So when we come back into the shelter of the presence of God and move even more deeply into his heart—into the secret place of El Shaddai—we find ourselves once again in the realm of Eden. As we become adept in our communion with God, we move even more deeply into Eden for the solace, care, and safety we need. A world of wonder and beauty is calling.

5.

The Turning of the Heart

In an experience which often transcended all their
powers of expression, [the mystics] realized God as
an abiding Fact, a living Presence and Love, and by
this their whole existence was transformed.
And this happened to them, not because He loved and
attended to them more than He does to us, but because
they loved and attended to Him more than we do.

EVELYN UNDERHILL, *MYSTICS OF THE CHURCH*

Jesus told a beautiful story about a lost son turning for home. It
spoke so deeply into the human psyche that it became one of the
most beloved of all Christ's parables. The story essentially goes
like this:

A selfish and self-centered young man, the younger of two
brothers, desperately wanted to get out from under his father's
traditions, to break free into a new way of living. He begged his
father to give him his half of the inheritance early, and the father,
heartbroken, relented. The son took off that very night.

He found the freedom he was looking for in another country and spent every dollar he had on drugs, prostitutes, and parties. The moment he went bankrupt a famine hit that land, and in one day this very lost son was reduced to something less than a migrant worker. Impoverished and exiled, he had nothing to eat, no place to stay; he slept with pigs in their filth. This young man was destitute in every way—body, soul, and spirit.

Reality, however, can be a very good tutor.

He remembered his father's estate—how even the hired hands had food and shelter, a place to call home. He came back to himself, and in that very hour he turned toward home (based on Luke 15:11–20).

He turned for home; I think that's the part that speaks so deeply to the human heart. We are all looking for home. Humanity is in exile, and we are feeling threadbare in the soul.

Trauma can help us appreciate the depth of these gospel stories more than we have. The young man is homeless; that is traumatizing. He is hurled into poverty; that, too, is traumatizing. He suddenly finds himself on the streets in a foreign country, destitute. That is brutal on the human heart.

Notice that his turning was first a turning of the heart, before his feet took one step. He *remembered* his father's estate—he remembered home, and his heart turned there. We see this turning of the heart in many places in the Scriptures, like in David's psalms:

TRAUMA CAN HELP US APPRECIATE THE DEPTH OF THESE GOSPEL STORIES MORE THAN WE HAVE.

"My heart says of you, 'Seek his face!' Your face, LORD, I will seek" (Psalm 27:8).

This isn't a poetic expression; David means it literally. As an ordinary mystic who became a mature mystic, he is seeking the face of his God with all his heart.

And remember—David was a hunted man. He often had to hide in severe wilderness conditions from his pursuers, who would kill him in an instant if they found him, just like many persecuted people groups today.

Harriet Tubman had to hide from her enemies as she guided slaves to freedom along the Underground Railroad during the American Civil War. Her stories sound a lot like David's; she, too, was a mystic because she heard the voice of God, trusted it completely, and followed him through many dangers: "'Twasn't me, 'twas the Lord! I always told Him, 'I trust you. I don't know where to go or what to do, but I expect you to lead me,' an' He always did."[1]

In times of desolation, David turned to God with all his heart and found him to be his true refuge before anything in his circumstances changed:

> O God, you are my God;
>> I earnestly search for you.
> My soul thirsts for you;
>> my whole body longs for you
> in this parched and weary land
>> where there is no water.
> *I have seen you* in your sanctuary
>> and gazed upon your power and glory.
> Your unfailing love is better than life itself. (Psalm
>> 63:1–3, emphasis added)

The mystic can access God anywhere; this is very good news. This was the secret of the beautiful life of Brother Lawrence, known for his book *The Practice of the Presence of God*:

> I cannot imagine how religious persons can live satisfied without the practice of the presence of God. For my part I keep myself retired with Him in the depth of the centre of my soul as much as I can; and while I am so with Him I fear nothing; but the least turning from Him is insupportable.[2]

The maturing mystic is not satisfied with anything short of union with Christ. This is what our humanity was made for and this is what Christ invites us into: "I have given them the glory that you gave me, that they may be one as we are one—I in them and you in me" (John 17:22). "Then they'll be mature in this oneness" (John 17:23 THE MESSAGE).

Don't worry; this will come to you over time. Especially through the practice I'm about to share.

Turning Toward Jesus

One of my favorite Gospel stories takes place on Easter morning; it centers around Mary Magdalene. Heartbroken, devastated, Mary has gone to the tomb of Jesus to grieve, but his body is no longer there. Most of you have experienced grief; it is concussive, debilitating. Mary can hardly breathe, and her eyes are so drenched with tears she mistakes the risen Christ for the gardener:

> Now Mary stood outside the tomb crying. As she wept, she bent over to look into the tomb and saw two angels in white, seated

where Jesus' body had been, one at the head and the other at the foot.

They asked her, "Woman, why are you crying?"

"They have taken my Lord away," she said, "and I don't know where they have put him." At this, she turned around and saw Jesus standing there, but she did not realize that it was Jesus.

He asked her, "Woman, why are you crying? Who is it you are looking for?"

Thinking he was the gardener, she said, "Sir, if you have carried him away, tell me where you have put him, and I will get him."

Jesus said to her, "Mary."

She turned toward him and cried out, "Rabboni!" (John 20:11–16)

She turned toward him. It is one of the best lines in all of Scripture. In her trauma and grief, she turns to face Jesus.

I adore this story for so many reasons. Jesus chose Mary Magdalene—a single woman he invited into his inner circle, something no rabbi at that time would have even considered. He chose this very special friend of his to appear to on Easter morning before anyone else. Even before Peter and John. This is so beautiful I cry every time I read it.

It is a very mystical story, by the way. Mary speaks to angels; she sees the resurrected Christ and speaks with him as well. It is all reported as quite normal. So we will have to include Mary Magdalene among the first of the famous Christian mystics. She is experiencing the Kingdom and its King.

Jesus simply says her name, "Mary!" And she turns.

That is all we need to do as well. This is the basic practice of learning to take refuge in God, this turning of the heart. The practice is closer, simpler, and more accessible to you than you might think.

You certainly know what it's like to turn your heart *away* from someone. A friend hurts you, a spouse or parent says something terribly wounding, and in that moment your heart withdraws. It turns away. *I'm not sure I can forgive you for that.* We all have experienced this sort of turning many times over.

But we can also turn our hearts *toward* someone.

You arrive at a bus station in a foreign country; you are hoping your friend has gotten the time right and is going to meet you. It's crowded, hot, and you don't speak the language. You feel alone and vulnerable. It's a dangerous city, you've been warned. Then, across the platform, you see your friend making their way toward you. Before you can cry out their name, your heart has leapt toward them.

Your little ones are playing with the neighborhood children outside. Suddenly you hear a crash of some sort, then tears and a cry that needs no further explanation: "Mommy!" Your heart is in an instant fully and completely turned in the direction of your child as you dash out the door.

We always turn before we turn, friends. The heart turns and the body follows.

> WE ALWAYS TURN BEFORE WE TURN, FRIENDS. THE HEART TURNS AND THE BODY FOLLOWS.

Mystics and Pragmatic Skeptics

Back to the question my friend asked: "Yes, but how do I love God? How do I take refuge in him? I mean, *practically* speaking?"

I have compassion for the question, but friends—this is the mind-set learned from pragmatic materialism, from being Disciples of the Internet. We honestly believe the practical question is the most realistic, the most helpful. It is not true, but this mind-set currently rules nearly all Christian preaching and teaching; it rules the publishing industry and the pulpit. *Make things simple. Break it down into steps.* Of course, there are practices every saint has relied upon through the ages to develop their amphibious life with God; we will explore those. But this obsession with "break it down and make it practical" is something else altogether. For example, over the past several decades I have watched the Church become utterly infatuated with marriage seminars offering all sorts of tips and techniques for couples. But what about the deeper underlying issues, the issues of heart and soul? When you rely on techniques alone, you kill the very essence of love.

A client came to me in distress over her marriage. She was confused, confounded, and heartbroken. Her husband was faithful and observed all the right techniques—remembering her birthday, flowers on their anniversary. But there was no genuine intimacy. His heart and soul were completely absent. It was crazy-making. In terms of the practical steps, he was a good husband. But he was utterly failing the very heart of marriage. It was like being married to a laptop.

Notice that when Scripture addresses marriage, it does so with reverence for the deep mysteries:

> There are three things that are too amazing for me,
>> four that I do not understand:
> the way of an eagle in the sky,
>> the way of a snake on a rock,

the way of a ship on the high seas,
>   and the way of a man with a young woman.
>   (Proverbs 30:18–19)

Creation, no less than marriage, is a wild and mysterious realm. It doesn't function like your printer. Our obsession with the practical is an attempt to get control over the mystery. But that is not how God made the world. The buyer for a paper mill walks through a forest seeing only cubic feet of pulp; the mystic and child are filled with wonder and communion. For them, the sunset speaks a different language than Google does—so, too, the wind in the trees and every river flowing to the sea. The heart learns lessons there that are far truer than any barren fact. As the mystic (and mathematician) Blaise Pascal wrote, "The heart has its reasons that reason knows not of."

If you give a child an ice cream bar, they will run to sit down in a favorite place and unwrap it, then relish it, happy feet swinging beneath them, a child's version of a dog wagging its tail.

Hand the same bar to an adult and they will flip the wrapper over, inspecting the number of calories, the contents, the carbs-to-protein ratio. By then all joy is gone. We have got to get out of this terrible way of operating in the world and especially with God. Your heart knows how to turn to him and love him. It doesn't need the latest neuroscience to be enabled to do so. Lay down the skeptic; take up the mystic.

I named Thomas Aquinas in the roster of the great mystics; that might have surprised some of you, for he is mostly remembered for his theological brilliance. But Thomas knew and experienced Jesus profoundly, and he used his brilliance to demonstrate that true knowledge is *experiential* knowledge of God:

The word *scientia* can designate an intellectual discipline, but it can also denote a direct, experiential type of knowing, a sort of knowledge through contact and touch. In what amounts to a delightful play on words, Thomas is telling us that the academic science of theology is drawn from the direct experience (*scientia* in the second sense) of God that is had by God himself and by the "blessed," those saints who are now enjoying the vision of God in heaven. He means that the science of sacred doctrine is a kind of participation in the inner life of God.[3]

Let's Practice

"Turn to God with all your heart," wrote Thomas à Kempis, "and Christ will come to you." First thing every morning, I pray something like this before I do anything else:

I run to you this morning, Father. I run to you this morning, Jesus. I hide myself in you. I run into your refuge, Lord.

And it happens; it takes place in the hidden realm.

As you learn to be an ordinary mystic, ask the Holy Spirit for his help:

Holy Spirit, help me turn to Jesus.
Help me run to the Lord for refuge.
Help me to hear his voice.
I ask you to open my spiritual vision and hearing;
tune my heart to your presence.
Take me into the shelter of the Most High.

As you grow in this practice, it will become the doorway into the intimacy, communion, and refuge your soul longs for. I want you to turn to Christ with your heart, right now. Turn away from all that holds your attention and turn toward Jesus with your heart.

You can turn to Jesus by your side or you can turn to Jesus who dwells within you. He's always right there. Give your heart's attention to him. Give your heart's affection to him.

Say out loud,

My heart, turn toward Jesus; turn toward Jesus.

Shortly you will find him. As you do, move toward him and come "into" him, for he is your refuge. You might be helped by saying to him,

Jesus, I love you. I love you. I love you, Lord.

And then,

I come into you, Lord. I run into you. I come into you, Lord Jesus.

You may only feel a sense of peace or well-being. You may feel much, much more. Eventually you will learn to see him, hear him, come into him.

Practice this before feelings change; practice it before you experience much at all. Sometimes I have to turn, and turn, and turn until I become aware of Jesus. It helps me to imagine myself turning my back on the world and facing Jesus only.

In fact, it seems counterintuitive, but you will find this practice of "turning" most helpful when you turn with that part of your heart that is not doing well—the part that is feeling anxious or sad, lonely or lost. With that very part of your heart, turn toward Jesus. Turn in his direction. Run toward him. Come into him.

Let's try it again . . .

My heart, turn toward Jesus; turn toward Jesus; turn toward Jesus.

As if he were right there (and he is), turn toward him with all your heart. Move toward him, come "into" him, for he is your refuge.

Jesus, I love you. I love you. I love you, Lord. You are my refuge.

I come into you, Lord. I run into you. I come into you, Lord Jesus. You alone are my refuge.

Remember now—the ordinary mystics down through time experienced God deeply, profoundly, "not because God loved and attended to them more than He does to us, but because they loved and attended to Him more than we do."

PAUSE

Take a few deep breaths.

    Gently remind your soul what you are learning.

    It helps to say it out loud.

6.

The Myth of Neutrality Versus
the Consecrated Life

Society—which meant pagan society—limited by
the horizons and prospects of life in "this world"—
was regarded by them as a shipwreck from which
each single individual had to swim for his life.

THOMAS MERTON ON THE DESERT FATHERS,
THE WISDOM OF THE DESERT

The mighty refuge psalm, Psalm 91, has a *progression* to it. First
comes the promise:

Those who live in the shelter of the Most High
will find rest in the shadow of the Almighty.

Then, a recitation of the many ways that El Shaddai will protect
us. Rescue from every trap and protection from deadly disease, the
terrors of night, the arrow that flies by day. Oh to experience it! How
humanity needs this in such a wicked hour.

Nine verses in, there comes a critical turning point:

> If you make the LORD your refuge,
>> if you make the Most High your shelter,
> no evil will conquer you. (verses 9–10)

That "if" is revelatory.

The refuge of God and his Kingdom is only for those who choose to take part in it. This fact is so irritating to human nature. We just want to get on with our life and have God cover us. That's not quite how things work.

> "I am the true vine, and my Father is the gardener. He cuts off every branch in me that bears no fruit, while every branch that does bear fruit he prunes so that it will be even more fruitful. You are already clean because of the word I have spoken to you. Remain in me, as I also remain in you. No branch can bear fruit by itself; it must remain in the vine. Neither can you bear fruit unless you remain in me." (John 15:1–4)

Hmmm . . . Jesus is laying out conditions for a flourishing life. Were you aware there were conditions?

He goes on,

> "I am the vine; you are the branches. If you remain in me and I in you, you will bear much fruit; apart from me you can do nothing. If you do not remain in me, you are like a branch that is thrown away and withers; such branches are picked up, thrown into the fire and burned. If you remain in me and my words remain in you, ask whatever you wish, and it will be done for you." (verses 5–7)

There is that irritating "if" again. *If* we remain in him, the refuge and resources of God are ours.

Here is the simple fact: You can choose to leave the protection of God. People do it all the time. You can choose to live within God and his Kingdom refuge, or you can choose to live outside of it.

> HERE IS THE SIMPLE FACT: YOU CAN CHOOSE TO LEAVE THE PROTECTION OF GOD. PEOPLE DO IT ALL THE TIME.

"Remain in me," Jesus urges. You can almost hear the plea in his voice: *Stay in Me; don't operate in anything outside of me.* But we are stubborn creatures, we humans.

I Did It My Way

We didn't intentionally wander out from the refuge of God one spring break, but wander we did, and the trip turned out to be an unmitigated disaster.

This was back in the days when we still had two teenage boys at home. Our routine for spring break had become an annual flight from winter each March, which in Colorado is still thoroughly snowy and cold. But routines can be tricky; they are not foolproof. Our practice was to do some listening prayer and move into a plan where we felt we had God's blessing. Something within the refuge of God.

But this particular year, every time we prayed about spring break, we heard nothing. Crickets. That should have been enough warning to at least hit the Pause button and wait for clarity. But human nature is like a toddler with car keys; we want our way and often we can get it. So we simply went ahead and booked a trip. We chose a beach city in Florida, booked a house, booked flights. And from the moment we hit the ground, everything went sideways. First, we got lost. Second, when we finally did reach our rental, it was nowhere near a beach. The weather was terrible, with a howling wind. And, to top it all off, city maintenance crews were pulling up the sewer lines directly in front of the house we rented. Demolition equipment hammered away dawn to dusk.

I think Jesus was silent when we asked about the trip because he was trying to slow the momentum down, bring us to a place of yielded submission. He doesn't force people into his refuge; he wants us to choose it for ourselves.

There Is No Neutral Ground

A bad vacation is nothing. People choose careers God never intended them to pursue; they marry spouses they should never have married. We make all sorts of decisions that are simply based on what we want to do. The consequences of living outside the refuge of God can be devastating. You have seen it for yourself.

I know this is disruptive, but we must mature as adults in God's care, so let's explore for a moment a little ontological orientation to the worldview of the Bible, the worldview of Jesus.

For this reason, since the day we heard about you, we have not stopped praying for you. We continually ask God to fill you with the knowledge of his will through all the wisdom and under- standing that the Spirit gives, so that you may live a life worthy of the Lord and please him in every way: bearing fruit in every good work, growing in the knowledge of God, being strengthened with all power according to his glorious might so that you may have great endurance and patience, and giving joyful thanks to the Father, who has qualified you to share in the inheritance of his holy people in the kingdom of light. For he has rescued us from the dominion of darkness and brought us into the kingdom of the Son he loves, in whom we have redemption, the forgiveness of sins. (Colossians 1:9–14)

This is a powerful prayer. God longs to bless us, strengthen us, guide us. He truly does. What I want you to notice is found in the last sentence: "For he has rescued us from the dominion of darkness and brought us into the kingdom of the Son he loves, in whom we have redemption, the forgiveness of sins."

The passage is describing the best human migration possible, from one kingdom to another, from slavery into the refuge of God. Now, how many kingdoms are named here? Only two: the Kingdom of God and the kingdom of darkness. From God's perspective there are only two kingdoms or "countries" in this universe. Did you see any other options mentioned here? There is God's Kingdom or Satan's. That's it. Those are your choices.

GOD LONGS TO BLESS US, STRENGTHEN US, GUIDE US.

I think this will be something of an epiphany for most of you.

And let's not forget, those kingdoms are at war with one another. Psalm 91 is set in the context of war, as are the rest of the refuge psalms, as is the entire biblical narrative. Oh, we live in a love story, friends. A love story set in a world at war. The mystic says, *How thrilling! What an amazing invitation! I want to live as deeply into God's country as I possibly can!*

Most human beings, however, think they have found a third option and a third location—a sort of Switzerland of neutral human existence where people who don't particularly want God or don't want to go to the effort of living in his Kingdom get to carry out their lives in relative peace. That third option appears to be what Scripture calls The World.

The World is where most of the human race has chosen to go on with their lives. They work, marry, have families, raise their children, and vacation in a shared agreement that The World is a reasonably safe place for human beings and an entirely successful alternative to God and his Kingdom. The delusion is truly supernatural when you simply take the data on human existence outside the protection of God and his Kingdom. Those anxiety rates don't indicate human wellness. People do not flourish outside of God— not for long, not in ways that are lasting and true.

Has your experience of The World been one of sweet refuge?

Do you know what high schoolers face in The World of school these days—even private schools? The sexual chaos, drug culture, gender deconstruction, the bullying, violence, and shootings? They are swimming in a toxic, condensed version of The World. What could possibly be the explanation when young girls have, in a three-year period, experienced a 5,000 percent increase in gender dysphoria? No sociologist or psychologist can explain such a dramatic explosion.[1]

The World is hard on the human heart—very hard.

But human nature is a stubborn thing. Our refusal to live within the kindness of God's created reality is then pushed further into the creation of alternative realities like the metaverse, where you can be anyone and do anything you like. Mark Andreessen, the man credited with creating and popularizing a large part of the Internet, blatantly confessed,

The vast majority of humanity lacks Reality Privilege—their online world is, or will be, immeasurably richer and more fulfilling than most of the physical and social environment around them in the quote-unquote real world.

The Reality Privileged, of course, call this conclusion dystopian, and demand that we prioritize improvements in reality over improvements in virtuality. To which I say: reality has had 5,000 years to get good, and is clearly still woefully lacking for most people; I don't think we should wait another 5,000 years to see if it eventually closes the gap. We should build—and we are building—online worlds that make life and work and love wonderful for everyone, no matter what level of reality deprivation they find themselves in.[2]

This is The World as we currently have it—humanity in full flight from reality, fully persuaded there is an alternative space in which to live out our chosen narratives, whether that space is online or simply in the re-creation of reality in our minds.

But then we run into this exposé in the first epistle of John:

We know that anyone born of God does not continue to sin; the One who was born of God keeps them safe, and the evil one cannot harm them. We know that we are children of God, and that the whole world is under the control of the evil one. (1 John 5:18–19)

The World as we envision it—society, culture, commerce, the arts—is under the power of the evil one, meaning it is under his jurisdiction, his rule, his sway. Which means this world that we so often perceive as relatively neutral is actually an extension of the kingdom of darkness. This reality is truly disruptive, even for many followers of Jesus.

I don't think I would need to convince you of this if you were a Jew living in Nazi Germany or a Christian living in an Islamic regime. But many small European countries were hoping to remain neutral in the early stages of World War II, countries like Belgium and Czechoslovakia. Their fragile delusion evaporated when Hitler's forces rolled in and swallowed them up in a day.

Now I know, I know—The World does not *present itself* as particularly evil most of the time (depending on where you live and operate at a given moment in human history). It is so brilliantly crafted, The World seems to offer everything a person could want. Yes, it is filled with pressures and the pace of life is utter madness, and yes—there's the injustice. But most of the time there's just enough comfort and distraction to keep us pacified. It is a trap crafted with ancient cunning and malice.

But The World is the puppet of the evil one. Listen to James, the brother of Jesus, on The World: "Don't you know that friendship with the world means enmity against God? Therefore, anyone who chooses to be a friend of the world becomes an enemy of God" (James 4:4).

If we are going to live with a clear-headed sobriety, with adult maturity, we need to come to terms with the fact that there are only two kingdoms and no third (or fourth or fifth) option, and certainly no neutral ground. As C. S. Lewis would write, "There is no neutral ground in the universe: every square inch, every split second, is claimed by God and counter-claimed by Satan."[3]

Which is why the mystics and all who would be like them seek to live a consecrated life. Why else would the great Saint Athanasius have been nicknamed by his peers Athanasius Contra Mundum (Latin for "Athanasius Against the World")?

The Exquisite Beauty of a Consecrated Life

IF WE ARE GOING TO LIVE WITH A CLEAR-HEADED SOBRIETY, WITH ADULT MATURITY, WE NEED TO COME TO TERMS WITH THE FACT THAT THERE ARE ONLY TWO KINGDOMS AND NO THIRD (OR FOURTH OR FIFTH) OPTION, AND CERTAINLY NO NEUTRAL GROUND.

"Therefore, I urge you, brothers and sisters, in view of God's mercy, to offer your bodies as a living sacrifice, holy and pleasing to God—this is your true and proper worship" (Romans 12:1). Our bodies are a very practical expression of something "under our rule," something that belongs to us in immediate proximity. We have a say over our bodies in terms of what we eat, what we drink, who we have sex with, etc. And we are urged by God to *present our bodies to him* in an act of consecration.

"Consecration" is choosing to dedicate something to Jesus to be his and his alone. The Hebrew word is *qadash*, directly related to the word *qodesh*, which means "holy." Biblically speaking, the first act of consecration takes place on the seventh day of creation in Genesis 2:3, when God blesses and sanctifies the Sabbath day. From that point on, consecration becomes the precondition for God's filling something. You can consecrate your body (and please, your sexuality), your money, your time, your dreams and aspirations.

The refuge life is a consecrated life, which is to say we choose to bring our lives and all that is under our care into God's Kingdom and under the rule of Jesus.

AND WE ARE URGED BY GOD TO *PRESENT OUR BODIES TO HIM* IN AN ACT OF CONSECRATION.

Now, of course, consecration is both an act and a lifestyle. We choose to dedicate our bodies to God, and then we live that decision out as we operate in holiness in our sexuality, our appetites, and how we treat our bodies (we are not allowed to abuse them). The same holds true for anything "in our kingdom," anything under our direct supervision.

So, for example, my morning prayers begin this way:

My dear Lord Jesus—I come to you now to be restored in you, renewed in you, and to receive your Glory, Love, and Kingdom. I love you, Jesus. I love you, Lord. I take refuge in you. And I give myself to you completely—heart and soul, mind and strength, body temple, spirit. I cleanse myself with your Blood—heart and soul, mind and strength, body temple, spirit. I ask your Holy Spirit to restore me in you, restore our union, and fill this time of prayer. Restore our union, Lord. Restore our union.

We will get back to morning and evening prayer later in the book. For now, I simply want to point out that each and every morning I consecrate in prayer all that is "me" in order to bring myself fully back into union with Jesus and under his rule. This is the "if" of Psalm 91 and John 15—I am choosing the refuge of God.

Later in the prayer I go on to bring "all things of my kingdom" under the rule of Jesus and into his Kingdom. (Remember now, there is no neutral ground; you do not want anything under your jurisdiction wandering out from the jurisdiction of Jesus.)

This is the first act of a consecrated life.

I like the phrase "under your rule and into your Kingdom" because I want all things in my domain, all of the things that I have say over, *completely* situated under the jurisdiction of Jesus and into his Kingdom.

There is, of course, much more that follows in a consecrated life. Our choice of entertainment. The way we respond to people. What we fantasize about. Behavior matters. Choices matter. But you must start somewhere. And that somewhere is learning to consecrate things, to bring them under the jurisdiction of the Lord Jesus Christ and into his Kingdom.

The maturing mystic lives with sober awareness and seeks over time a fully consecrated life. This is the doorway into life as it was meant to be; it is our first step back toward the paradise refuge of Eden.[i]

Breathe

Back to the vacation.

Even though my wife and I know all these things and believe them, even though we have experienced the choice of living within the refuge of God and drinking from his river of delights, we wanted on that particular spring break to act as though there *are* neutral choices. To behave as though we could simply do what

---

i. For a bit more on the consecrated life, see chapter 6, "Unconverted Places," in my previous book, *Resilient*.

we wanted to do. It did not go well because it was not grounded in reality.

I called it an unmitigated disaster, but that is not entirely true. God is immensely gracious and kind. He is always forgiving. And even when we wander out from under the shelter of the Most High, he will do his best for us while not sparing us the valuable lessons we need. There were moments of joy on the trip, moments of laughter. We made jokes about how bad it all was. We put on noise-canceling headphones to deal with the construction outside the house.

God is still our good Father even when we play the prodigal.

My goodness, if you knew the actual scope and depth of the predatory forces of the kingdom of darkness prowling this world, bent on the destruction of humanity, and if you could see the billions of poor choices human beings make every day, exposing them to those predatory forces, you would see the breathtaking abundance of God's goodness. This is what the reformers called "common grace." There is still kindness, provision, and protection extended even to those who are in full flight from God. "For he gives his sunlight to both the evil and the good, and he sends rain on the just and the unjust alike" (Matthew 5:45 NLT).

> EVEN WHEN WE WANDER OUT FROM UNDER THE SHELTER OF THE MOST HIGH, HE WILL DO HIS BEST FOR US WHILE NOT SPARING US THE VALUABLE LESSONS WE NEED.

But friends, you do not want to push your chances on this.

You do not want to put yourself in a lifestyle constantly needing God's rescue from your poor decisions. From an unconsecrated life. And we do not want to blame God for the repercussions of an unconsecrated life either. The shelter is there. The refuge is there. His "country" is an entirely wonderful place in which to live, if we will accept the constraints. If we will bring all things under his rule and into his Kingdom.

PAUSE

Breathe.
  Linger a moment.
  Reflect.

———o———

We are pursuing the life of ordinary mystics growing toward maturing mystics—not because it is something curious and new, but because we need help and healing; we need rescue and refuge; we need guidance and provision.

All of that and more are available to those who practice returning to, and abiding in, the refuge of God.

7.

Taking Refuge in the Truth

All at once I felt that I had been born again and entered
into paradise itself through open gates. Immediately
I saw the whole of Scripture in a different light.

MARTIN LUTHER

The killer whale looked at me intently with a huge, unblinking eye, bright with intelligence and a sort of intense interest that unnerved me. It was the cold, calculating interest of an apex predator, and he seemed way too interested in *me*. We were not far apart—fifteen feet perhaps. The pod of orcas accompanied by this chieftain among males had come cruising past our fishing boat. A female orca and her calf swam by first, and the effect was enchanting. Magical. Everyone was taking photos.

Then the big male came up, his three-foot dorsal fin completely out of the water, and the piercing eye sized me up. Was he calculating the distance? My lizard brain told me, *You are about to be eaten. You are going to die.*[i]

---

i. The "lizard brain" refers to the limbic part of your brain; it is in charge of primitive impulses like fight or flight, and it needs refuge in order to turn off.

In truth, my family and I were quite safe. The boat we had chartered was built to handle Alaskan storms. The deck sat high above the surface, surrounded by a four-foot steel wall separating us from the orcas. I was safe. I truly was.

But *being* safe and *feeling* safe are not the same thing, and this difference can really shake the human soul.

I should add that *feeling* safe and actually *being* safe are not necessarily grounded in reality either. Alex Honnold may have felt safe free-climbing El Capitan with no rope or protection whatsoever, but one slip would have killed him. As C. S. Lewis wrote, "Perfect love, we know, casteth out fear. But so do several other things—ignorance, alcohol, passion, presumption, and stupidity."[1]

> *BEING* SAFE AND *FEELING* SAFE ARE NOT THE SAME THING, AND THIS DIFFERENCE CAN REALLY SHAKE THE HUMAN SOUL.

The Cycle Continues

We had a home. It was a garden paradise in the land of Eden, more beautiful than the most breathtaking places on earth, filled with laughter and holy wonder. Our hearts were free, bold, and true. We spoke with God; angels and all sorts of heavenly beings were our neighbors. We lived and worked in the garden temple of our God. It was a refuge unlike any other. From that place we were to venture out, bringing Eden to all the world.

We lost that refuge by listening to the lies of our enemy, the evil one whom Jesus called "the father of lies" (John 8:44).

Now the serpent was more crafty than any of the wild animals the LORD God had made. He said to the woman, "Did God really say, 'You must not eat from any tree in the garden'?"

The woman said to the serpent, "We may eat fruit from the trees in the garden, but God did say, 'You must not eat fruit from the tree that is in the middle of the garden, and you must not touch it, or you will die.'"

"You will not certainly die," the serpent said to the woman. "For God knows that when you eat from it your eyes will be opened, and you will be like God, knowing good and evil."

When the woman saw that the fruit of the tree was good for food and pleasing to the eye, and also desirable for gaining wisdom, she took some and ate it. She also gave some to her husband, who was with her, and he ate it. . . .

So the LORD God banished [them] from the Garden of Eden. . . . After he drove [them] out, he placed on the east side of the Garden of Eden cherubim and a flaming sword flashing back and forth to guard the way to the tree of life. (Genesis 3:1–6, 23, 24)

The trauma of this cannot be overstated; this is the child wrenched from its mother's arms by terrorists, the teenage refugee alone in a foreign country. You would think that the utter heartbreak of this would have inoculated the human race with everlasting resolve against it ever happening again.[ii]

If only. If only.

---

ii. In fact, scholars point out that the trauma of exile structures the entire Old Testament narrative. Tim Mackie and John Collins, "The Jewish Exile: How It Made the Bible," February 1, 2018, in *BibleProject Podcast: Exile*, episode 1, produced by Dan Gummel and Jon Collins, podcast, MP3 audio, 42:00, https://bibleproject.com/podcast/jewish-exile-how-it-made-bible/.

But each and every day, people continue to surrender the refuge of God by listening to the deceptions of the enemy and his puppet The World.

Every time you pick up your phone, turn on the news, get online, or simply step out into The World, a host of competing narratives rush to seize your attention. The battle right now is for your attention, folks. Billions of dollars are spent learning how to arrest your particular attention for three seconds, hoping you will click and enter into the "more" they want to offer. AI is watching and learning, watching and learning your every choice, so as to precisely serve up to you the tidbit you simply can't refuse.

Whatever is vying for your attention, it's pretty safe to say it isn't assuring you of the goodness of God, his active involvement in the world, and how utterly safe you are in his care.

Remember now—you are the disciple of the system that tutors you, the place you turn to on a daily basis for your understanding of the world. Which makes nearly all of us Disciples of the Internet and, we should add, social media (most people get their news these days from social media). However you get your information, it's pretty safe to say that source isn't feeding you the narrative of God, and so it's pulling you *away* from the refuge of the truth. There are only two kingdoms, friends, and no neutral ground.

Which kingdom are you listening to?

We've grown so accustomed to allowing The World to shape us, inform us, we hardly notice anymore. God is incidental, hardly mentioned in the hours of screen time we spend each week. My readers enamored with "the neuroscience" will find this fascinating: Neuroscientist Uri Hasson was one of the first academics to observe in the brain what we have always seen in the person: when we listen to someone's story, we quite literally become like them.[2] Yikes.

Earlier in this book I talked about the Internet's seductive erosion of confidence that we can ever really get to the truth of anything. The constant rebuttal and reversal of yesterday's facts has diminished our capacity to believe anything with wholehearted confidence. We are so skeptical, but we need something to fall back on, so we revert to our feelings.

"I feel, therefore I am." This emotivist understanding of the self shapes the way in which individuals participate and communicate in societal life. In the contemporary context, as Jean Bethke Elshtain observes, "all points seem to revolve around the individual's subjective feelings—whether of frustration, anxiety, stress, fulfillment. The citizen recedes; the therapeutic self prevails."[3]

> **IF GOD DOESN'T *FEEL* NEAR, WE CONCLUDE HE MUST NOT *BE* NEAR, WHATEVER SCRIPTURE MIGHT SAY.**

We fall back upon our feelings; emotions rule the day. If God doesn't *feel* near, we conclude he must not *be* near, whatever Scripture might say. If we don't feel we can find his refuge, we conclude we aren't safely tucked within it. Living feeling to feeling pulls us further into the wilderness.

No, You're Not

More corrosive than all of these are the personal assaults of the enemy's lies whispered to our hearts. They are far more brilliant than AI and utterly precise in their tailored messages to us. The evil one knows your story, your hurts and fears, your every vulnerability.

Against our loving God, who gave his own life for us, Satan always says something to the effect of "No, he's not."

God isn't good, or he wouldn't have let that happen.
God isn't with you; you are on your own.
God isn't listening to your prayers.
God isn't near to you; he's somewhere else.

Against your own heart Satan always undermines your identity, just as he tried to do with Jesus during his wilderness trial. "No, you're not" is his essential message.

You're not seen.
You're not safe.
You're not forgiven.
You're not a loving person.
You're not going to be okay.

On and on it goes. You know very well the personal version of this, the voices you wake to in the night or first thing in the morning.

Dear sons and daughters of the Living God, you cannot talk yourself out of this poison. You must shut this assault down just as Christ showed you when he countered Satan's lie upon lie with truth upon truth.

The devil said to him, "If you are the Son of God, tell this stone to become bread."

Jesus answered, "It is written: 'Man shall not live on bread alone.'"

The devil led him up to a high place and showed him in an instant all the kingdoms of the world. . . . "If you worship me, it will all be yours."

Jesus answered, "It is written: 'Worship the Lord your God and serve him only.'"

The devil led him to Jerusalem and had him stand on the highest point of the temple. "If you are the Son of God," he said, "throw yourself down from here. For it is written:

"'He will command his angels concerning you
    to guard you carefully;
they will lift you up in their hands,
    so that you will not strike your foot against a stone.'"

Jesus answered, "It is said: 'Do not put the Lord your God to the test.'" (Luke 4:3–5, 7–12)

And with that, Satan left.

You don't reason with demons; you silence them with the truth.

Lingering Attention

Oh, the joys of those who do not
    follow the advice of the wicked,
    or stand around with sinners,
    or join in with mockers.
But they delight in the law of the LORD,
    meditating on it day and night.

> They are like trees planted along the riverbank,
>> bearing fruit each season.
> Their leaves never wither,
>> and they prosper in all they do.
>> **(PSALM 1:1–3 NLT)**

This happy, happy tree—planted riverside, always nourished, always fruitful, never withering. The psalm is speaking about the possibilities for your *humanity*. It sounds almost Edenic, and it is meant to trigger that association. In the book of Revelation, when John sees the City of God come to earth and Eden restored, the Tree of Life is planted by the river—always bearing fruit, leaves always green and healing! We are meant to become like the Tree of Life!

The mystic heart will leap to this. *Oh please, Lord—yes! Show me that life!*

Like Psalm 91, Psalm 1 is utterly realistic; it presents two conditions toward becoming that happy tree:

- We detach ourselves from the culture around us and its narratives.
- We give *lingering attention* to the truth of God's word in the Scriptures.

This is the person who turns off the news, podcasts, and especially the political commentary and instead listens to the audio Bible during their commute or carpool.

The Hebrew word for "meditate on" literally means "to mumble." The Scriptures are meant to be texts that we quietly read aloud to ourselves over and over again, so that they work their way into our very being. We give God's instructions our lingering attention. This is the "if" of Psalm 91—*if* you will make the Most High your refuge. This is part of how that "if" gets played out in our lives. Those who are walking in the way of Jesus develop habits by which they give lingering attention to the truth as given to us by God.

What are your habits that allow you to give lingering attention to the truth?

> **IF YOU WANT THE REFUGE OF GOD, YOU TAKE THIS VERY SERIOUSLY.**

Remember friends—we surrendered our first refuge home by giving way to a lie, and we have come home by returning to the truth. Not merely a fact, but he who is the way, the truth and the life.

This back and forth, this war over the soul losing refuge by believing lies and returning to refuge by coming back to the truth, plays out every day of our lives. If you want the refuge of God, you take this very seriously.

Daily Proclamation

Let me suggest for you one practice that is sustainable and very fruitful: the daily declaration, or proclamation, of essential truths.[iii]

Returning to Psalm 91, notice the importance of the second verse:

> Those who live in the shelter of the Most High
> > will find rest in the shadow of the Almighty.
> *This I declare about the* LORD:
> He alone is my refuge, my place of safety;
> > he is my God, and I trust him. (NLT, emphasis added)

---

iii. Any spiritual practice that is not sustainable will fade away; you have to choose patterns you can maintain.

"This I declare." The psalmist is making a proclamation, and a very important one.

Declarations are both reminders to the soul and acts of defiance against the enemy's constant lies. Of this verse Spurgeon wrote, "To take up a general truth and make it our own by personal faith is the highest wisdom . . . to say he is *my* refuge, is the essence of consolation."[4]

What I'm strongly suggesting is this: Before you head out the door into your day, after your morning prayers, take a few more moments to declare out loud,

God is my Father.
I am his son (or daughter).
I am loved.
I am chosen.
God is my refuge.

And so on.

This counters the narrative assaults of The World, the cunning lies of our enemy, and it is also how we get out of the madness of allowing our feelings to dictate what is true and false for us. The saints and mystics through the ages held this to be an essential part of our fight for refuge.

Notice that Saint Patrick's famous "Breastplate" prayer begins with these lines:

I arise today
Through a mighty strength, the invocation of the Trinity,
Through belief in the threeness,
Through confession of the oneness
Of the Creator of Creation.

"Through confession," meaning through declaration and proclamation. He goes on to both remind himself and draw upon the work of Christ for him:

> I arise today
> Through the strength of Christ's birth with his baptism,
> Through the strength of his crucifixion with his burial,
> Through the strength of his resurrection with his
>   ascension,
> Through the strength of his descent for the judgment of
>   Doom.[5]

Seize this practice for yourselves, dear ones. I think you'll find it very helpful to keep a list of essential truths in your journal, on your desk, perhaps taped to the refrigerator or bathroom mirror.

What Truths to Proclaim?

I suggest you create a short list because, in order for any spiritual discipline to be helpful, it has to be sustainable. And your attention span has been eroded by technology, so be kind to yourself.

The list ought to contain both essential and personal truths. The essential ones are those core to the narrative God is telling.

- God is in control.
- He has not abandoned the human race.
- The story of God has been, is now, and always will be the story of the world.
- Jesus Christ will never leave me nor forsake me.

And perhaps

- I am a Christian mystic; God's presence and his Kingdom are completely available to me, and I experience them.

But I think your list should also include those truths that are particular to the places you are vulnerable, to buttress your heart and soul against the enemy's *No, you're not*. What are the biblical truths that counter the lies the enemy brings against you?

If it is shame you struggle with, you might declare each day:

> *There is no condemnation now for those in Christ Jesus.*
> *I am the righteousness of God in Christ.*

If it is fear, you declare,

> **God has not given me a spirit of fear but of power, love,**
> **and a sound mind.**
> *I am no longer a slave to fear but a child of God.*

Like that.

Confession: I typically don't *feel* I need to pause and do my declarations; often the practice is irritating because I just want to get on with my day. (The Way of Jesus runs up against our Self-Life all the time, and that's a very good thing.) But if I stop and linger with my declarations, saying them out loud to myself (and any other being that happens to be listening), I realize how much I need them, for they set me free, strengthen me, bring joy, bring me back to God and his refuge!

And when I say I'm declaring them out loud, I don't mean I am stating them once, like reading a list. I say them over and over again until I am back "in" them and the truth is back "in" me. Only then is it refuge in the truth.

The nineteenth-century mystic George MacDonald was born into Scottish Presbyterianism and trained as a Presbyterian minister—not a place known to be kind to Christian mysticism. But he had a poet's heart, and he loved Jesus deeply. C. S. Lewis in turn loved MacDonald deeply, and I find it significant that when Lewis created a book of MacDonald quotes for publication, he began with this one:

> That man is perfect in faith who can come to God in the utter dearth of his feelings and desires, without a glow or an aspiration, with the weight of low thoughts, failures, neglects, and wandering forgetfulness, and say to Him, "Thou art my refuge."[6]

God is your refuge. You are safe in him. You are. Feelings are important, but they don't get to determine reality. In this apostate hour, with so much skepticism and unbelief trying to get into our hearts and souls, we take our defiant stand and proclaim the truth even without the support of our feelings. This was a primary suggestion of Evagrius Ponticus in *Talking Back*—refute the enemy's lies with truth from Scripture:

> In the time of struggle, when the demons make war against us and hurl their arrows at us [cf. Eph 6:16], let us answer them from the Holy Scriptures, lest the unclean thoughts persist in us, enslave the soul through the sin of actual deeds, and so defile it and plunge it into the death brought by sin.[7]

This is the way to victory, and the means by which we stay in the refuge of God.

PAUSE

Take a few deep breaths.

Reflect.

Before you go on to the next chapter, begin your list of declarations right now.[iv]

_____

iv. In appendix 4 I include Neil Anderson's "Who I Am in Christ" list; Stasi and I have used it for years. I encourage you to draw upon it but, nonetheless, still make your declarations your own.

8.

The Breastplate of Patrick

I bind to myself today
the strong power of the invocation of the Trinity:
The faith of the Trinity in the Unity
The Creator of the elements.
I bind to myself today,
the power of the Incarnation of Christ, with that of his Baptism,
The power of the Crucifixion with that of his Burial,
The power of the Resurrection with the Ascension,
The power of the coming of the Sentence of Judgment.

SAINT PATRICK

These words are from an early translation of the famous Breastplate of Saint Patrick, one of the missionary Christian mystics who risked life and limb to bring the Gospel of Jesus to the warring Celts of Ireland. In these opening lines, Patrick is taking refuge in God in a mighty way. *I bind to myself* has a fierce intention to it, and no small wonder—these monks were operating in a dangerous pagan world, where witchcraft, shamanism, human sacrifice, curses, Celtic chieftains, and warring clans were the daily context of their mission.

A situation much like that of Psalm 91; a context much like ours.

The disciples of Patrick and other early Celtic saints took daily prayer very seriously, for they saw it as their way of taking refuge in God. From the 700s to 900s *anno domini*, Irish monks developed a particular kind of prayer called the "lorica," the Latin word for armor. (The Latin Vulgate—a late-fourth-century Latin translation of the Bible—uses the word "lorica" for "breastplate" in Ephesians 6:14.) And so, over time, Patrick's *lorica* was named his "Breastplate."

But it has an earlier and more significant name.

In another early collection of those Celtic Christian prayers, the *Liber Hymnorum*, Patrick's prayer is entitled *Faeth Fiada*, which in Old Irish means "The Deer's Cry" or the "Mist of Concealment." For it was passed down that Patrick's prayers of refuge were so powerful as to conceal him from those witches and pagan warlords, cloaking Patrick in the semblance of a deer that he might pass in safety. Not unlike Brother Andrew smuggling Bibles into Soviet Russia while praying, "Lord, in my luggage I have Scripture that I want to take to your children across this border. When you were on Earth, you made blind eyes see. Now, I pray, make seeing eyes blind. Do not let the guards see those things you do not want them to see."[1]

This is the dynamism of Psalm 91—refuge in the midst of danger, shelter in times of war.

The Work of Christ as a Mighty Tower

I bind to myself today,
the power of the Incarnation of Christ, with that
of his Baptism,
The power of the Crucifixion with that of his Burial,

The power of the Resurrection with the Ascension,
The power of the coming of the Sentence of
Judgment.[2]

These saints and mystics did far more than give reverent thanks to God for his goodness; they sought deep *personal participation* in the work of Jesus Christ. We must do the same.

The spiritual warfare of the hour we are living in is no different than what Patrick and his disciples faced. It might be worse because of the lateness of the hour, and it can be withering when you are under it. In those desolate moments, when my heart feels abandoned by God and I want to cry out, *Where are you, God? Why aren't you doing something?* I catch myself and protect my heart like a breastplate by declaring that he *has* intervened for us in the mightiest and most powerful of all ways.

God has intervened for us with such thorough and everlasting victory in the work of Jesus Christ—his Cross, Resurrection, and Ascension.

I don't think most postmoderns understand this, or they feel far from it, but the mystic heart *runs* to take refuge here, in the fact that we have already been included in the Cross, Resurrection, and Ascension.

> **I PROTECT MY HEART LIKE A BREASTPLATE BY DECLARING THAT HE *HAS* INTERVENED FOR US IN THE MIGHTIEST AND MOST POWERFUL OF ALL WAYS.**

I have been crucified with Christ and I no longer live, but Christ lives in me. The life I now live in the body, I live by faith in the Son of God, who loved me and gave himself for me. (Galatians 2:20)

But God is so rich in mercy, and he loved us so much, that even though we were dead because of our sins, he gave us life when he raised Christ from the dead. (It is only by God's grace that you have been saved!) For he raised us from the dead along with Christ and seated us with him in the heavenly realms because we are united with Christ Jesus. (Ephesians 2:4–6)

What greater fortress could we ask for than this? What greater deliverance? A new life, a new identity, to be situated with Christ right now in the heavens, in his authority? Father—thank you! Thank you, God! We take refuge in it! Show us how to actively *participate* in it!

And so my daily prayers also include an invocation like Patrick's:

> *Jesus, thank you for coming to ransom, restore, re-create, and reinstate me. I love you, Lord. I worship you. I receive again this morning all the work and triumph in your Cross. I take my place in the Cross today, dying with you to sin and the Self-Life, to Satan, to The World and its corruptions. I take up the Cross and crucify sin and the Self-Life. I bring the Cross, Blood, and sacrifice of the Lord Jesus over my life today, over my home and household. I cleanse myself with the Blood of Christ.*
>
> *And Jesus, I also sincerely receive you as my life. You are my life. I am saved by your life. I reign in life through your life. I receive all the triumph in your resurrection, and I take my place in your resurrection this morning. I enter your life, Jesus, and I receive your faith, hope, and love. I receive your wisdom, power, and strength. Your holiness. Your life in me. And I bring the resurrection and the River of Life over,*

around, and throughout my life today, my family, and my household.

Jesus, I also receive all the work and triumph in your authority, ascension, and throne. All authority in the heavens and on this earth has been given to you, Jesus. You are the Integrating Center of all things. And I have been raised with you in your authority. So I take my place in your authority and ascension now, and I bring all of my home, family, and household under your rule and into your Kingdom. I command the fullness of your Glory, Love, and Kingdom throughout my kingdom and domain this day.

It helps, my skeptical friends; it works . . . mightily.

The Clean Sea Breezes of the Centuries

Let's return to a more robust version of "The Deer's Cry" as a way of nourishing our starving postmodern souls.

Imagine yourself in a wild land of ancient forests, howling wolves, and bloodthirsty pagan warriors who would delight to cut your throat or sell you into slavery if they found you wandering in the wilderness. There are few roads and no cities at all—only small farms and villages. You are in a hermitage, huddled by the fire in the wee hours before dawn with a handful of Christ-followers. The wind in the trees seems to carry on it the voices of witches chanting spells and curses. Against *you*. What the new day holds, only heaven knows.

Together you recite this prayer:

I arise today
Through a mighty strength, the invocation of the Trinity,
Through belief in the threeness,
Through confession of the oneness
Of the Creator of Creation.

I arise today
Through the strength of Christ's birth with his baptism,
Through the strength of his crucifixion with his burial,
Through the strength of his resurrection with his
	ascension,
Through the strength of his descent for the judgment
	of Doom.

I arise today
Through the strength of the love of Cherubim,
In obedience of angels,
In the service of archangels,
In hope of resurrection to meet with reward,
In prayers of patriarchs,
In predictions of prophets,
In preaching of apostles,
In faith of confessors,
In innocence of holy virgins,
In deeds of righteous men.

I arise today
Through the strength of heaven:
Light of sun,
Radiance of moon,

Splendor of fire,
Speed of lightning,
Swiftness of wind,
Depth of sea,
Firmness of rock.

I arise today
Through God's strength to pilot me:
God's might to hold me,
God's wisdom to guide me,
God's eye to look before me,
God's ear to hear me,
God's word to speak for me,
God's hand to guard me,
God's way to lie before me,
God's shield to protect me,
God's host to save me
From snares of devils,
From temptations of vices,
From everyone who shall wish me ill,
Afar and anear,
Alone and multitude.

I summon today all these powers between me and those
        evils,
Against every cruel merciless power that may oppose my
        body and soul,
Against incantations of false prophets,
Against black laws of pagandom,
Against false laws of heretics,

Against craft of idolatry,
Against spells of witches and smiths and wizards,[i]
Against every knowledge that corrupts man's body
    and soul.

Christ to shield me today
Against poison, against burning,
Against drowning, against wounding,
So that there may come to me abundance of reward.
Christ with me, Christ before me, Christ behind me,
Christ in me, Christ beneath me, Christ above me,
Christ on my right, Christ on my left,
Christ when I lie down, Christ when I sit down, Christ
    when I arise,
Christ in the heart of every man who thinks of me,
Christ in the mouth of everyone who speaks of me,
Christ in every eye that sees me,
Christ in every ear that hears me.

I arise today
Through a mighty strength, the invocation of the Trinity,
Through belief in the threeness,
Through confession of the oneness
Of the Creator of Creation.[3]

My hunch is this doesn't sound at all like your morning prayers, for you are a postmodern materialist and the early Celtic Christians

---

i. "Smiths" is referring to blacksmiths, who in ancient cultures were often considered magicians or witches, in part because they often crafted idols and various tokens for dark purposes.

were childlike mystics who went on to become mature mystics by necessity. They lived at a time when the heavens and earth were inseparable. Historian Thomas Cahill called Patrick "a Christian druid, a man of both faith and magic."[4] Truth for him was no sterile fact; it was a living, breathing reality, full of power and passion, wild and free. He was Chesterton's ideal mystic, with one foot on earth and the other in heaven.

> DO YOU SEE THAT THESE EARLY SAINTS FULLY ACCEPTED THAT THE POWERS OF GOD AND HIS KINGDOM WERE THEIRS TO ABSORB AND INVOKE?

"The Deer's Cry" cited above was no doubt improved upon by Patrick's disciples and their disciples after them. But this version is thoroughly Irish, steeped in Celtic Christianity.

Do you see that these early saints fully accepted that the powers of God and his Kingdom were theirs to absorb and invoke?

I arise today
Through the strength of Christ's birth with his baptism,
Through the strength of his crucifixion with his burial,
Through the strength of his resurrection with his
    ascension. . . .
Through the strength of the love of Cherubim,
In obedience of angels,
In the service of archangels.

They assume the presence of evils like witchcraft, and they also assume they can personally invoke the mighty powers of heaven against it:

> I summon today all these powers between me and
> those evils,
> Against every cruel merciless power that may oppose my
> body and soul,
> Against incantations of false prophets,
> Against black laws of pagandom,
> Against false laws of heretics,
> Against craft of idolatry,
> Against spells of witches and smiths and wizards,
> Against every knowledge that corrupts man's body and
> soul.[5]

Let us not forget that these early mystics thoroughly converted a pagan land into a thriving Christian kingdom, and from there they brought Christianity back to a Europe in utter ruins after the fall of Rome. They were *victorious*, friends!

Various renditions of the central verses of "The Deer's Cry" still hang in many Irish kitchens today:

> Christ with me, Christ before me, Christ behind me,
> Christ in me, Christ beneath me, Christ above me,
> Christ on my right, Christ on my left,
> Christ when I lie down, Christ when I sit down, Christ
> when I arise.

If we prayed this, and believed it, we would find refuge indeed.

Later in this book we are going to get to morning and evening prayer. I share "The Deer's Cry" here to open the window and give you a whiff of the sea, what Lewis called "the clean sea breeze of the centuries."[6] It is a tonic from a mystic thoroughly grounded in

Christian theology, that can help you untangle yourself from the skeptical pragmatism that has been your food day and night since birth.

I think you should go back and read "The Deer's Cry" out loud, praying it, *declaring* it as you do.

PAUSE

Breathe.

Linger.

Did you go back and say "The Deer's Cry" out loud?

9.

Lions, Cobras, Scorpions

Never wound a snake; kill it.

HARRIET TUBMAN

We are shifting now from the ancient forests of Celtic Ireland to the even more ancient deserts of the Judean wilderness four hundred years earlier.

The Judean Desert is a famously wild and desolate place. It's hotter and drier than the Sahara (averaging less than four inches of rain a year). Summer temperatures hover around 104 degrees Farenheit. This is David's "dry and weary land where there is no water" (Psalm 63:1 AMP). Wadis and canyons tear the landscape apart, plunging at times more than a thousand feet into narrow ravines. Scorpions and snakes seem the only creatures fit for this wilderness. The deadly painted carpet viper lives there, as does the extremely venomous Israeli mole viper (whose venom is both a cardiotoxin and a neurotoxin, far more fatal than rattlesnake venom).

If you knew where to hide, it was a truly insurmountable fortress.

David fled there many times; this is no doubt the "stronghold" he speaks of in Psalm 18, for once he was safe in that wilderness, no bounty hunters could find him:

> The LORD is my rock, my fortress and my deliverer;
>   my God is my rock, in whom I take refuge,
>   my shield and the horn of my salvation, my
>   stronghold. (Psalm 18:2)

And it was into this same furnace that the Spirit led Jesus for forty days, to prepare for and engage in direct confrontation with Satan himself (heaven-and-earth combat that mystics like Saint Anthony, Patrick, and Luther would later understand).

Jesus, full of the Holy Spirit, left the Jordan and was led by the Spirit into the wilderness, where for forty days he was tempted by the devil. He ate nothing during those days, and at the end of them he was hungry.

The devil said to him, "If you are the Son of God, tell this stone to become bread."

Jesus answered, "It is written: 'Man shall not live on bread alone.'"

The devil led him up to a high place and showed him in an instant all the kingdoms of the world. And he said to him, "I will give you all their authority and splendor; it has been given to me, and I can give it to anyone I want to. If you worship me, it will all be yours."

Jesus answered, "It is written: 'Worship the Lord your God and serve him only.'"

The devil led him to Jerusalem and had him stand on the

highest point of the temple. "If you are the Son of God," he said, "throw yourself down from here. For it is written:

> "'He will command his angels concerning you
>   to guard you carefully;
> they will lift you up in their hands,
>   so that you will not strike your foot against a stone.'"

Jesus answered, "It is said: 'Do not put the Lord your God to the test.'"

When the devil had finished all this tempting, he left him until an opportune time. (Luke 4:1–13)

The story and dialogue are terse, calculating, and cryptic. Did you notice that the evil one threw Psalm 91 in Jesus' face? Of all the Scriptures Satan could have used, why Psalm 91?

Many scholars believe it had to do with the role of the psalm in Jewish tradition, which was carried forward into the early church:

> Psalm 91:5–6 was read persistently as a promise that God protects the faithful from demonic attacks. Among the psalm fragments from the Dead Sea Scrolls, for example, a variant form of Psalm 91 is attested in a collection of four songs, possibly intended to exorcise demons. The inclusion of Psalm 91 in it suggests that it, too, has served as a protection against demons.[1]

Jesus is going to draw a direct connection between Psalm 91 and his instructions to his disciples a few chapters later in Luke. He knew what this psalm meant, and apparently so did his enemy.

The Gospel of Luke also attests to the first-century use of this psalm against demons. In Luke 10:19, Jesus appoints seventy of his followers and confers on them the assurance of Ps 91:13 ("On lion and viper you tread"). When they return, they report back to Jesus, "Lord, in your name even the demons submit to us!" (Luke 10:17). For Luke, those who receive the assurance of Psalm 91 derive from it the power to ward off demons.[2]

The early church clung to Psalm 91 as a breastplate against the enemy. Engravings of the psalm or portions of it have been found on early medallions, pendants, rings, and the doorposts of Christian houses.[3] It is possible that Jesus may have been declaring Psalm 91 during his prayers in the wilderness.

The Unseen Realm of Darkness

Let's return to that gripping scene in the Judean wasteland. Imagine Jesus walking around his desert camp, fasting, praying, quoting Scripture, and no doubt declaring aloud Psalm 91, "El Shaddai is my refuge and fortress . . ."

It's interesting to know that El Shaddai can be translated *God of the wilderness*:

While the traditional English translation of Shaddai is based on the Greek . . . , the Hebrew epithet Shaddai (שדי) has been understood by most scholars as deriving either from "mountain" (Akkadian *šadû*) or "field/wilderness" (Hebrew שדה). Hence, El-Shaddai should more correctly be understood as the "God of the Mountains" or the "God of the Wilderness."[4]

"You are with me in the wilderness, God of the wilderness; you are my stronghold, God of the mountain crags."

Now picture the evil one circling Jesus' camp like a leopard or panther, just outside the firelight, watching intently, listening to the man he does not yet fully understand as the incarnate God declaring Psalm 91 aloud. I believe this is why Satan throws it back in his face:

> For he will command his angels concerning you
>> to guard you in all your ways;
> they will lift you up in their hands,
>> so that you will not strike your foot against a stone.

Folks, the very next verse foretells his downfall:

> You will tread on the lion and the cobra;
>> you will trample the great lion and the serpent.

Clearly, *clearly* the reader is meant to understand the lions and cobras of Psalm 91 to refer to foul spirits. Satan knew that he was the very serpent Psalm 91 promises victory over, for he was the serpent in the garden that Almighty God promises would be crushed by a coming messiah! Was he provoking Jesus, trying to see if he would make a premature move? Quoting it back to Jesus to taunt him?

The important thing to know about Psalm 91 is that Jews and Christians have seen the psalm as a direct weapon against demonic attack. Jesus went on to draw the direct connection for his disciples and make its application perfectly clear: "I have given you authority to trample on snakes and scorpions and to overcome all the power of the enemy; nothing will harm you" (Luke 10:19).

Crushing Not Binding

Remember now—we are maturing in our understanding of how we actively *participate* as ordinary mystics in God as our refuge and stronghold; these passages are critical to God's provision for us. "Trampling and crushing" are active and definitive movements—there is nothing passive here at all.

But of course.

You're standing in the kitchen of your home one evening, doing dishes. Your toddler is playing on the floor nearby, when out of the corner of your eye you spot a scuttling movement on the tiles. You quickly turn to see a scorpion crawling toward your child, claws out in crablike fashion, poisonous tail raised to strike. How would you handle the moment?

> "TRAMPLING AND CRUSHING" ARE ACTIVE AND DEFINITIVE MOVEMENTS—THERE IS NOTHING PASSIVE HERE AT ALL.

You would stomp on it.

You would crush it without a moment's hesitation.

This is the promise, the assurance and the *directive* of our Lord Jesus on how we are to deal with foul spirits. It sounds a whole lot like Patrick's Breastplate!

> I summon today all these powers between me and
> those evils,
> Against every cruel merciless power that may oppose my
> body and soul,
> Against incantations of false prophets,
> Against black laws of pagandom,

Against false laws of heretics,
Against craft of idolatry,
Against spells of witches and smiths and wizards,
Against every knowledge that corrupts man's body
and soul.

We probably ought to admit that this is very different from the usual attitude taken by most followers of Jesus toward demonic assault (and "every cruel merciless power"). Most folks want to ignore spiritual warfare. The simple proof: How often do you pray directly against foul spirits? If it's rarely, you're ignoring it.

But we are looking for the refuge of God, and he makes it clear that crushing the serpent is essential to finding shelter and staying in it. If a scorpion was scuttling across the floor to your toddler, you would not think twice; there would be no hesitation. You would stomp on it, making your home a safe place again.

This is probably a good point in our journey to talk about authority and commanding "in the name of Jesus." Christ has made it very clear that he has given his authority to us, and it is *we* who will "trample on snakes and scorpions and . . . overcome all the power of the enemy" (Luke 10:19). In a healthy home, the parents take care of nearly every task for their infant child—they feed them, clothe them, tie their shoes. Over time, more and more responsibility is entrusted to the maturing child—they pick their own clothes, feed themselves, tie their own shoes. The same is true as we mature as sons and daughters of God.

God our Father could communicate the Gospel to every human consciousness without human assistance; but he chooses to entrust us with much of that task. He could meet the needs of the poor without our involvement, but here again he prefers to engage us. We have a role to play. The same is true when it comes to spiritual warfare and, as we will see later, "taking hold of" the many resources of heaven for our aid. A good example can be seen in this story from the book of Acts:

> Once when we were going to the place of prayer, we were met by a female slave who had a spirit by which she predicted the future. She earned a great deal of money for her owners by fortunetelling. She followed Paul and the rest of us, shouting, "These men are servants of the Most High God, who are telling you the way to be saved." She kept this up for many days. Finally Paul became so annoyed that he turned around and said to the spirit, "In the name of Jesus Christ I command you to come out of her!" At that moment the spirit left her. (Acts 16:16–18)

Notice that Paul does not ask Jesus to make the foul spirit leave. He uses the authority of Christ entrusted to every disciple in Luke 10:19 to do the commanding himself. It is very direct, forceful, and effective.

I think this is going to help many sincere Christians with the violent language throughout the Psalms and their bold cry for devastating judgment on "my enemies."

> Arise, LORD!
> > Deliver me, my God!
> Strike all my enemies on the jaw;
> > break the teeth of the wicked. (Psalm 3:7)

> In Your mercy cut off my enemies,
> And destroy all those who afflict my soul. (Psalm 143:12 NKJV)

It's hard to reconcile this brazen hostility with "love your enemies and pray for those who persecute you" (Matthew 5:44). That is, until we understand the fuller picture given to us in Ephesians by the mystic Saint Paul: "For our struggle is not against flesh and blood, but against the rulers, against the authorities, against the powers of this dark world and against the spiritual forces of evil in the heavenly realms" (Ephesians 6:12).

Every mystic understands the true nature of the battle we are in; our true enemies are not people—they are foul spirits. Calling down judgment on those spirits is an entirely different matter. Which brings us back to Psalm 91 and Jesus' use of it in Luke 10—*we* will trample on these foul beings; *we* will crush them.

Thus my morning prayers also include this paragraph:

> *In the name of the Lord Jesus Christ I now command the Cross, Resurrection, and Ascension of Jesus Christ against the forces of darkness attacking me and my household this day—all foul spirits, powers, and devices; all forms of black arts. Fire and Glory to destroy our enemies, in the name of the Lord Jesus Christ. I ask the heavenly host to carry out these orders now and to rebuild the canopy of protection around my home. To guard and protect us this day. Your Fire around us, Father, and your Glory within.*[i]

Active Participation

God is our refuge, absolutely. Right now.

---

i.   Fire and Glory are from Zechariah 2:5, which we will dive into in a coming chapter.

He does send his angels to protect us, far more than we know. The angels assigned to protect you are with you every day.

But as we have seen, our *participation* in the refuge is required, and this includes using the mighty victory of Christ against the assaults of the enemy. The refuge is there; the victory is there. Our role is to enforce it, with force.

Friends, it's as simple as this: If you wake in the night to a palpable fear tormenting you, sit up and command,

> THE REFUGE IS THERE; THE VICTORY IS THERE. OUR ROLE IS TO ENFORCE IT, WITH FORCE.

In the name of the Lord Jesus Christ, I order all foul spirits of fear to the feet of Jesus Christ immediately; if you refuse to leave, I call down judgment from Almighty God upon you.

If you are dogged by shame and accusation, stop and command,

In the name of the Lord Jesus Christ, I renounce all accusing spirits right now. "There is no condemnation for those who are in Christ Jesus." I order every accusing spirit to the feet of the Lord Jesus Christ immediately; if you refuse to go, I call down judgment from Almighty God on you right now, in Jesus' name!

Thinking back to those stone towers that dot the coasts of the British Isles—they were built against marauding enemies, slave traders, and deadly Viking raiders. The folks of that hour took their situation seriously. We live in a world just as dangerous. Too many good people neglect this essential part of discipleship to Christ. Please take this seriously.

I will help you flesh this out in the next chapter as we learn to take refuge in the love of God.

PAUSE

Take a deep breath.

Let it settle in.

If someone asked you to tell them about this chapter you've just read, what would you say to them?

10.

Love as Refuge

For you bless the godly, O Lord;
you surround them with your shield of love.

KING DAVID

You are safe and secure in the refuge of God. That is the major theme.

The minor theme is the war raging outside, which we do need to take seriously. The enemy is arrogant, and he loves to intimidate us by making the war seem like the major theme. It is not. So let's return to love.

All who declare that Jesus is the Son of God have God living in them, and they live in God. We know how much God loves us, and we have put our trust in his love. God is love, and all who live in love live in God, and God lives in them. And as we live in God, our love grows more perfect. (1 John 4:15–17)

This is breathtakingly beautiful. God our refuge is unassailable love; as we intentionally choose to live in love, we secure ourselves within God and his refuge.

So I often find myself praying,

I take refuge in Your love, Jesus.
I take refuge in Your love.
Surround me with Your love.
Shield me with Your mighty love.

This, too, is an essential part of daily prayer, for we live in an hour of swirling hatred on the earth. Do I really need to convince you of this?

Hutus kill Tutsis because they are Tutsis. Anti-Semites kill Jews because they are Jews. Serbs attempt to eradicate Bosnian Muslims; Bodos war against Indian Muslims. We could go on to name the bloodshed in places like Darfur, Iraq, Indonesia, Sri Lanka. Hatred is pandemic; it is poisoning human relations at every level. It's like it got into the water and the air, and we are all taking it into our systems.

Some time ago *Time* magazine ran the cover story "Why We're Losing the Internet to the Culture of Hate,"[1] and it's only gotten worse since then. Much, much worse. Try posting an opinion on politics, gender, race, border control—*anything*—and you will be met with a firestorm of hatred.

Have we forgotten Covid politics?

At the height of the Covid-19 pandemic, you could not even *whisper* a diverse opinion on vaccines, masks, quarantines, and such without explosive reactions, threat of job loss, expulsion from school, even imprisonment. Covid politics split families and churches in ways few things ever have; many local churches lost half their congregations. Forever. And in an hour like this, when people are raw, ragged, and running on fumes, it doesn't take much to set someone's sinful nature off. People are shooting others because of traffic offenses. There was a shooting in my town recently. A young man shot his roommate because he asked him to take out the trash.

These are incendiary times.

There is only one safe place in the madness.

We Must Take Refuge in Love

"God is love, and all who live in love live in God, and God lives in them" (1 John 4:16 NLT). We should clarify that John, one of Jesus' dearest friends, is talking about the kind of love we see God manifest in Jesus Christ. This is not an unhealthy, codependent love. This doesn't mean taking care of people far beyond what you should. The Greek word here is *agape*, designating God's sort of love, not *phileo* (brotherly love) or *eros* (romantic or erotic love). God's love is high and above fickle affection; it is unconditional but also jealous; it is unfailing but also insistent and fierce.

It is the love you see at the Cross.

God is this kind of love, and all who live in this kind of love live in God, and God lives in them. I don't think I can properly emphasize the importance of this refuge in a moment like ours.

You are provoked many times a day to take up some offense.

People offend without even knowing it. People wound without even knowing it. News is barely even news anymore; it is taking sides and placing blame. The enemy is watching and waiting for us to take the bait of offense; the moment we begin to harbor grudges or feel resentful, entertain negative thoughts and emotions, he then throws gasoline on the fire. Suddenly we are feeling strong emotions that overwhelm our commitment to love.

A consecrated life begins with a consecrated heart.

Our first refusal to leave the refuge of God is to give no place to hatred in our hearts or in our lives. When you live in a spiritual environment like the one I've been describing, you have to shut every door to hatred in your heart and soul. Simply, "no."

(Now, we are talking about hatred here, but we could add any corruption of heart and soul—pride, lust, rage, greed. A consecrated heart will help you against any violation of your purity and thus your place in the refuge of God.)

Do not take the bait of offense! Let no act, no word, no offense of any kind get you to give way to hatred, unforgiveness, resentment, bitterness. Do not let it in your heart!

Radical Forgiveness

On a practical level, you're going to need to practice forgiveness far more often than you think.

Someone cuts me off in traffic, and I now say, *I forgive you for that*. Someone sends me a snarky email, and I say, *I forgive you for that*. Someone, yet again, fails to come through in what they should have done. *I forgive you for that*.

Hatred has become so rampant we have to get radical with our forgiving. Forgive everything.

Over the past year, when I have come to Jesus about some offense real or imagined, he says to me, "Forgive everything. *Everything*."

He knows the hour; he knows what we must do to stay in his refuge. So I will often say out loud, "I forgive it all. I forgive everything." There's so much offense in a single day that you simply can't keep accounts. And you certainly can't wait for people to come back around and apologize. Let's practice a radical holiness (which is refuge) by simply forgiving everything.

I understand that sometimes it takes months, even years, for a person to come around to forgiveness. They might need the help of a therapist. But after the years have passed, they still find themselves where they started—needing to forgive everything. While the therapeutic process can be deeply helpful, the saints of ages past would also encourage you to *begin* with forgiveness too. Do it now, not later, so that you can come back into the refuge of God's love *and from that safe place* work through your hurts.

Stasi and I were shouting it aloud in our living room last night: "*We forgive everything!*"

Why shouting? Because we could feel the riptide of the undercurrent of hatred trying to get in through a myriad of offenses, and you don't talk your way out of this stuff. By shouting "*We forgive everything!*" we were slamming the door of our hearts shut to the invasion, the poison, and making it clear to the spiritual beings listening that we will give no ground to them.

I will often also command: "I kick all hatred out of my being. *Now!* In the name of the Lord Jesus Christ, I kick all hatred out of my being."

Protecting Love

Earlier in this book I was describing the way the Internet has worn down our capacity to trust and believe; the constant undermining of yesterday's facts has made skeptics of us all. Well, the culture of offense and hatred is doing the same thing—it wears love down. Jesus warned about this when he said,

> At that time many will turn away from the faith and will betray and hate each other, and many false prophets will appear and deceive many people. Because of the increase of wickedness, the love of most will grow cold, but the one who stands firm to the end will be saved. (Matthew 24:10–13)

Love is something we are going to have to firmly protect.

Now here is the problem—as soon as I say the word "love," many different things come to your heart and mind.

> *Oh great, now I have to take care of everyone.*
> *I guess I have to let my toxic mom back in.*
> *I don't get to have my own feelings about this; I just have to let everyone have theirs.*

We all have a story of love, how we learned love in the world. Most of those lessons confused our hearts and souls about the nature of love. We need to allow Jesus to heal our story of love as we take refuge in his love. So when I say we need to protect love, I am only talking about love as we see modeled in Jesus Christ. He has the ability to move *toward* people, move *against* people, and move *away* from people as true love guides him.

"And this I pray, that your love may overflow still more and more in real knowledge and all discernment" (Philippians 1:9 NASB). By all means, we need to be discerning in love. Sometimes that means distancing yourself from toxic people, setting healthy boundaries. But never out of cynicism, never in offense, and never in hatred. If love seems to be growing cold in your life, that should get your attention. Rush to protect it. I often pray,

> *Fill me with your love for this person, Jesus. Fill love in me with your love.*
> *Jesus, I need you to restore love in me.*

IF LOVE SEEMS TO BE GROWING COLD IN YOUR LIFE, THAT SHOULD GET YOUR ATTENTION. RUSH TO PROTECT IT.

Protecting love in your heart includes your love for God. Satan hates your love for Jesus and your Father; he will try to poison it. His favorite tools are suffering, chronic disappointment, or something that feels like God has betrayed or abandoned you. You must not let the enemy do this. So I have had to add this to my prayers as well:

> *I cleanse my love of God with the Blood of Jesus and the River of Life.*

I'll say more about the power of cleansing things with the Blood of Christ and the River of Life in a coming chapter; I mention it here because our love gets poisoned by The World and the enemy, and most people have never thought to cleanse it. But the mystic knows that when you do, your love is refreshed and renewed.

> "Because he loves me," says the Lord, "I will
> rescue him;
> I will protect him, for he acknowledges my name.

He will call on me, and I will answer him;
I will be with him in trouble,
I will deliver him and honor him.
With long life I will satisfy him
and show him my salvation." (Psalm 91:14–16)

Safety is in God; the people you find there happen to be the people who love and adore him.

I think God is also revealing to us that as we choose to love him, as we intentionally and deliberately turn our hearts and souls to him in the practice of love on a daily basis, he is better *able* to rescue us because of the culture of hatred around us. The person swimming away from the lifeboat is harder to save than the person swimming toward it.

God's love around us is paired with our choices to love, and that makes for beautiful refuge. That's part one.

Trample the Snakes and Scorpions

This insane hatred we are seeing in the world—the racial violence, the volatile politics, the cancel culture—what in heaven's name is going on here? Some dark, supernatural force filled with malice is operating behind the scenes, throwing gasoline on the fire of tense human relations.

Any astute reader of Scripture knows it is "evil rulers and authorities of the unseen world . . . mighty powers in this dark world, and . . . evil spirits in the heavenly places" (Ephesians 6:12 NLT).

Now yes, yes, yes—human sin is deadly. It alone would destroy the world if God did not restrain it. Absolutely. But given the volatile nature of the *spiritual* hatred released in the world, given its unrelenting commitment to steal, kill, and destroy, you are also going to need to *command* the love of God against all spiritual forces of hatred as a deliberate practice.

Pilgrims who ventured into the Egyptian desert to sit at the feet of Saint Anthony (the father of monasticism) would often hear from far off shouting coming from his hermitage. Anthony was rebuking foul spirits with force, trampling on snakes and scorpions. Like Stasi and me shouting, *"We forgive everything!"*

The background of that story that found us shouting in the living room was this: Some unexplained and rather surprising tensions sprang out of nowhere within our church fellowship, and we came home a little beat up and surprised at having to navigate it all. We knew at its core that it was spiritual warfare. However, even though we *knew* the enemy was involved, Stasi and I tried to talk it through over dinner instead of treating it as spiritual warfare, and it began to jump on us! Tension and misunderstanding began to multiply; we were slipping into conflict when I said, "Can we stop and pray about this?"

And here is how we prayed:

We renounce all hatred coming into our home right now. We renounce all spiritual forces of hatred trying to get into our marriage and into our ministry. We forgive everyone for everything. And we command the fire-love of Almighty God against all forces of hatred immediately. We cut them off with the mighty love of God, and we order them to the judgment of the Lord Jesus Christ immediately; if they disobey, we call down their immediate judgment in the name of the Lord Jesus Christ. No exceptions.

The atmosphere in the room changed in a moment.

All tension, misunderstanding, and acrimony vanished.

Stasi reached out her hand and took mine in hers across the table. "Thank you," she said. "You rescued me."

Folks, I know I keep repeating this, but it needs repeating: When spiritual warfare is present, you cannot talk your way out of it. You must shut it down.[i]

You Too

Now, you might be wondering, *Why did John call down the fire-love of God? What's that about?*

In Deuteronomy and in Hebrews we are reminded that our God is a jealous God, a consuming fire:

> Be careful not to forget the covenant of the LORD your God that he made with you; do not make for yourselves an idol in the form of anything the LORD your God has forbidden. For the LORD your God is a consuming fire, a jealous God. (Deuteronomy 4:23–24)

> Therefore, since we are receiving a kingdom that cannot be shaken, let us be thankful, and so worship God acceptably with reverence and awe, for our "God is a consuming fire." (Hebrews 12:28–29)

God's love is so passionate, so pure, so explosive, it is not merely

---

i. As Jon Tyson beautifully put it, this means "you are violent with the spirits who are opposed to God and you are gentle to people who are victims of them. Most people are violent with the people and they let the spirits off."

like a consuming fire—it *is* a consuming fire. It consumes everything unholy. A mystic I know told me that sometimes when she visits the heart of God in prayerful communion she sees fire all around!

And we should remember that many times in the Old Testament, when God promises to rescue his people, it is said he will come down as fire:

> The LORD reigns, let the earth be glad;
>> let the distant shores rejoice.
> Clouds and thick darkness surround him;
>> righteousness and justice are the foundation of
>>> his throne.
> Fire goes before him
>> and consumes his foes on every side. (Psalm 97:1–3)

Fire goes before our Jesus and consumes his enemies on every side. In a violent war like this, where foul hatred is coming against you every day of your life, you need to call upon his fire! When it comes to foul spirits, demonic hatred, and things like every cruel, merciless power that may oppose my body and soul, incantations of false prophets, black laws of pagandom, false laws of heretics, craft of idolatry, and spells of witches and smiths and wizards, by all means call down holy fire-love against it! Call down the consuming fire! Consume it!

A Consecrated Heart

Hebrews 12 ends with these verses: "Therefore, since we are receiving a kingdom that cannot be shaken, let us be thankful, and so worship God acceptably with reverence and awe, for our 'God is a consuming fire'" (verses 28–29).

Hebrews 13 *begins* with this verse; it follows directly after those above: "Keep on loving each other as brothers and sisters" (verse 1).

The chapter break is unhelpful; it is certainly out of place (as you know, those breaks were inserted centuries later). The flow of thought is clear—God is love—jealous love as Deuteronomy makes clear. Not petty jealousy but love that pursues us until we are like him in love. Our created destiny is that we shall, as John the Beloved promised, abide in the refuge of God's love because we are living it out in our lives:

> God is love, and the man whose life is lived in love does, in fact, live in God, and God does, in fact, live in him. (1 John 4:16 PHILLIPS)

Throughout the book we have been pressing deeper and deeper into what it means to take shelter in the refuge of God. Love is at the center. Of course it is.

So it comes as no surprise that the lives of maturing Christian mystics down through the ages are always marked by what loving, kind people they were. Kindness can be your guide through the day; be kind to people and, Francis would add, to animals and all living things. Be kind to the people who least deserve it.

And by the way, we must not allow hatred in, not even to

OUR CREATED DESTINY IS THAT WE SHALL, AS JOHN THE BELOVED PROMISED, ABIDE IN THE REFUGE OF GOD'S LOVE BECAUSE WE ARE LIVING IT OUT IN OUR LIVES.

ourselves. No indulging self-contempt of any kind. You must practice kindness to yourself, for the way you treat your own heart is the way you will end up treating everyone else's.

In this way we will carry about the refuge of God with us wherever we go.

PAUSE

Breathe.

Do you need to pray about something like I've modeled in the past two chapters?

11.

Jesus: The Integrating Center of All Things

We will begin, then, with the creation of the world and
with God its maker, for the first fact that you must
grasp is this: *the renewal of creation has been wrought by
the self-same Word Who made it in the beginning.*

ATHANASIUS, *ON THE INCARNATION*

We are seeking refuge as ordinary mystics growing into mature
mystics who recognize that the refuge of God is dynamic and
requires our participation—as when we consecrate our lives to God
daily, when we stay in the truth, or when we crush the scorpions
trying to harm us.

The refuge is always available; the refuge is something to be
seized.

I've made intentional references to trauma throughout the
preceding chapters because I do believe that humanity's deepest
need is to find how union with God can address even our trauma.

This is the epicenter of the book, this chapter and the next.

I began the book with these lines:

Faith has always been a fragile thing in the human heart. Precious, lifesaving, but fragile in the way a coral reef is fragile, or a newborn fawn in the woods. It is something to be *protected*.

I would say the same of your humanity—your humanity is a fragile thing also, and when that coral reef is bombarded with chemicals, or when that fawn must constantly run from forest fires, the effects are traumatizing. As a metaphor, this is our daily experience on the planet. If we are truly to find the full refuge of God and his Kingdom, we must find healing for the vulnerable and traumatized places within us.

Now don't get anxious; Jesus has you. The Gospel is truly gospel, for the soul is healed through union with Christ, and that is available to every person, anytime, anywhere.

De-creation or "Unmaking"

Turning and turning in the widening gyre
The falcon cannot hear the falconer;
Things fall apart; the centre cannot hold;
Mere anarchy is loosed upon the world.

W. B. YEATS

The above lines are taken from a poem entitled "The Second Coming," but Yeats didn't quite mean what you mean by that. He was a good poet but something of a nut, with strange beliefs. His life was not a model of discipleship to Jesus Christ. Nonetheless, Yeats saw something coming, as many poets have, and what he saw unraveling has played out in our times.

I have quoted the part of the poem that arrests me most:

> Turning and turning in the widening gyre
> The falcon cannot hear the falconer.

This is humanity, swirling further and further away from God and his refuge. Like the prodigal, we have wandered so far from the shelter of the Most High we no longer hear his call to come home. As a result,

> Things fall apart; the centre cannot hold;
> Mere anarchy is loosed upon the world.[1]

Things do fall apart; the center cannot hold—not only in society and culture, which we see coming apart all around us, but this unraveling is also taking place *within* us. I would call it the Hour of Fragmentation, the "unmaking" of all things. Here in our most dire need, the Gospel of Jesus is going to shine for you with utter brilliance.

"In the beginning," as Genesis tells us, God creates an ordered world out of "chaos." "In the beginning God created the heavens and the earth. Now the earth was formless and empty, darkness was over the surface of the deep, and the Spirit of God was hovering over the waters" (Genesis 1:1–2).

Putting things together with intricate beauty and order is the work of God. I find it delightful that the Hebrew word *shalom* means "complete" or "whole." As theologian Dr. Tim Mackie explains, "Shalom refers to something complex, with lots of pieces, that's in a state of wholeness, completeness." When used as a verb, *shalom* means, "to make complete or restore."[2]

The purposes of God are wholeness, completeness.

On the dark side, we can therefore see more clearly that Satan's aim is to destroy things, to bring about disorder, anarchy. To unmake the beautiful creation of God wherever he can. If you have watched anyone slowly die of cancer, you have seen the gruesome deterioration—the unmaking of their body. Perhaps you have watched an aging parent succumb to dementia—the unmaking of their mind as it withers into fragmentation. My father died this way; it is terrible to watch helplessly by.

Satan unmakes or *de*-creates the truth when he tells a lie. This is how the entire spiral of de-creation began, for when Adam and Eve believed the lie and followed it, all creation was plunged into de-creation. I could be wrong, but it appears to me that this process of the unmaking of God's beautiful creation has intensified and accelerated in this hour.

Mental health services are at an all-time high; never before have so many resources been available, and yet we are nowhere near catching up to the global need. Or we could point to the deconstructing so many young people have done with their faith. The problem is, few have gone on to reconstruct it; they are wandering outside the refuge of God in a twilight of unbelief and despair.

This is a tender subject for many, sometimes heartbreaking, but it's important that we look at the unmaking of gender because gender is named in Genesis as essential to human dignity; it is core to how we bear the image of God: "So God created mankind in his own image, in the image of God he created them; male and female he created them" (Genesis 1:27).

When we see so many young people questioning their gender, when we behold an agenda to *encourage* the dismantling of gender, we see a kind of unmaking here as well, the dismantling of the image of God in humanity. De-creation has reached the epicenter.

Trauma would be another graphic example, and even more widespread. Mental health professionals now understand that trauma fragments the mind and the self:

> The Structural Dissociation model . . . describes how the brain's innate physical structure and two separate, specialized hemispheres facilitate left brain–right brain disconnection under conditions of threat. . . .
>
> In each individual client, I could see that some parts were easier to identify with or "own" and some parts were easier to ignore or dismiss as "not me." Internally, the parts were in conflict.[3]

All this to say, to be a human being in this hour is to be stained glass—beautiful still in our brokenness, but fragmented nonetheless. How we heal human fragmentation is one of the critical questions of this moment. Maybe *the* question.

Now for the shining brilliance of the Gospel of Jesus Christ.

The Integrating Center

The Son is the image of the invisible God, the firstborn over all creation. For in him all things were created: things in heaven and on earth, visible and invisible, whether thrones or powers or rulers or authorities; all things have been created through him and for him. He is before all things, and in him all things hold together. (Colossians 1:15–17)

Knowing what we know now about the enemy's plan to de-create all things, especially our humanity, the phrase "and in him all things hold together" should leap off the page to us! What hope is being offered here? What joy is being stated with such simple confidence?!

A similar promise is made in the first chapter of the book of Hebrews:

> Long ago God spoke many times and in many ways to our ancestors through the prophets. And now in these final days, he has spoken to us through his Son. God promised everything to the Son as an inheritance, and through the Son he created the universe. The Son radiates God's own glory and expresses the very character of God, and he sustains everything by the mighty power of his command. (Hebrews 1:1–3 NLT)

Jesus sustains all creation by the mighty power of his command. Obviously, or Satan would have torn all creation to pieces long ago. Jesus—through whom all things were made—is currently, at this moment, holding all things together; he sustains all creation. The love, forbearance, and patience of this is breathtaking—the tenderness and care, not to mention the mighty power of it!

The Gospel is good news because the healing of our fragmented souls is available in Christ anywhere, anytime, to anyone in the world. "Through him all things were made and without him nothing was made that has been made."

Including you. Jesus Christ was intimately involved in your creation. He knows everything about you. That is why he can be so essential in our healing. He is the Integrating Center of all things, including your very being. As the fourth-century mystic Athanasius wrote in his beautiful essay *On the Incarnation*,

THE HEALING OF OUR FRAGMENTED SOULS IS AVAILABLE IN CHRIST ANYWHERE, ANYTIME, TO ANYONE IN THE WORLD.

The renewal of creation has been wrought by the self-same Word Who made it in the beginning.

The Word of God came in His own Person, because it was he alone, the Image of the Father, Who could recreate man after the Image.[4]

Salvation is *re-creation*. Such hope is contained in this simple idea. As the twentieth-century mystic Leanne Payne repeated over and over again, "The soul is healed through union with Christ."[5]

The mystic says, *This is the answer to everything! O Jesus— re-create all things in me.*

In the remainder of this chapter, I will explain how the healing power of re-creation works in damage done to the soul that doesn't reach the level of severe trauma; we will begin with the ordinary heartbreaks that we all experience so that we might understand the process. Then we will move into the healing of trauma itself in the following chapter.

Hold Me Together

Here I am! I stand at the door and knock. If anyone hears my voice and opens the door, I will come in. (Revelation 3:20)

Whatever the need within us might be, the basics are the same: we give Christ access, we invite him in. We seek union with Jesus in the damaged parts of us, for the soul is healed through union with

Christ. I want to explain the healing of fragmentation because the great Gospel opportunity in the world at this moment is the healing of trauma. But before we get there, let's take a few gentle steps in that direction.

DAMAGE

First, we acknowledge that not all wounding fragments the soul.

Unkind words can pierce us; hateful words can wound. It might hurt for a long time; those wounds need tending to. But they do not cause fragmentation. Your beloved grandmother dies. You grieve, but it doesn't fragment your soul in the way trauma does, especially trauma from when you were young.

Still, the soul is healed through union with Christ whatever level the damage might be, and as a practice you will love inviting Jesus into those places within you that need his care.

> *Lord, come into this piercing I received from those words spoken over me. Come and cleanse my heart here; minister wholeness and renewal to me. I invite you here. Restore our union.*

> *Jesus, come into my grief over losing my grandmother. Come into my grief, Lord. Meet me here. Comfort me and restore my heart in this place. I pray for union with you in my grief.*

He promised if we open the door he will come in—deeply, intimately. George MacDonald experienced this bliss and reported,

> When our hearts turn to him, that is opening the door to him; then he comes in, not by our thought only, not in our idea only, but he comes himself, and of his own will. . . .

This is the height of mystical experience, this union with Christ.

Thus the Lord, the spirit, becomes the soul of our souls, becomes spiritually what he always was creatively . . . his deeper creative soul, working on and with his creation upon higher levels, makes the *I* and *me* more and more his, and himself more and more ours; until at length the glory of our existence flashes upon us . . . and know ourselves alive with an infinite life, even the life of the Father; know that our existence is not the moonlight of a mere consciousness of being, but the sun-glory of a life justified by having become one with its origin, thinking and feeling with the primal Sun of life, from whom it was dropped away that it might know and bethink itself, and return to circle for ever in exultant harmony around him.

Then indeed we *are*; then indeed we have life; the life of Jesus has become life in us; the glory of God in the face of Jesus, mirrored in our hearts, has made us alive; we are one with God for ever and ever.[6]

O Jesus, yes, Lord. Please. Do this for each of us.

This world erodes our union with Christ on a daily basis. Learning the intentional practice of inviting Jesus back into those places most needing his healing presence, his healing *union*, is something you will come to treasure as one of your greatest intimacies with God.

THE PROCESS

Earlier this year I became aware of a cynical reaction to hope rising up from somewhere within me. I'd be in a conversation with a friend and they would express something they were excited about or looking forward to: a vacation, a promise from God. Part of me would silently respond, *Yeah, sure. Whatever.*

It concerned me, and I paid attention.

We suffered several significant losses in 2023, and I was aware of something hurt and angry inside. It was "located" in the "function" of Hope within me. I'm choosing these words carefully, because they will help you understand how to move into restoration when it is needed in a particular place in your heart and soul. Sometimes it is the function of Love that needs restoration in us; other times it might be the function of Joy. As you pay attention to your inner world, as you go into those rooms Teresa of Avila described in her book *The Interior Castle*, you are much better situated to invite Christ into these places and experience his healing.

Faith, Hope, and Love—the greatest virtues and forces in our lives—seem to suffer special assault in this war. I think most of us try to carry on, with Faith, Hope, and Love limping with us—flagging, failing; but it would be far better to get the healing presence of Christ into those places within us.

Faith, Hope, and Love have a location within your soul, a locus. You can find them rather easily simply by looking, for example, for your longing for love. Tune into your longing for love, and you will find where Love "lives" within you; then move toward it. From that place, it is far easier to open the inner door to allow Christ in.

I had a quiet evening to myself, so I began to pay attention to Hope within me. You can locate the function and locus of Hope in your soul by simply thinking about hope, wondering what you are hoping for, or heading straight toward the loss of hope within. You can even move straight toward despair, for it is trying to overcome hope within you.

I could feel the damage there, in the locus of Hope in me. It wasn't in Love; Love was doing well. It wasn't in the place of Faith, either; the heartache and damage were clearly resident in Hope in me. I intentionally moved toward the pain and cynicism within me; I paid attention to the function of Hope within my heart and moved toward it. And here is what I prayed:

> *Jesus—come into the place of Hope in me. Meet me in this place, Lord.*

As I'm praying this, I'm "moving toward" the pain and hurt. I'm moving toward where hope lives in my heart and soul. The Revelation 3:20 dynamic of opening the door works far better when we are resident there—not detached, dissociated, operating from afar.

Jesus responded with a question: "What are you feeling here?"

> *I feel hurt and angry.*

The tears began to come.

> *I feel cynical and I don't want to be cynical.*

Jesus continued, "Invite me in. Love me here."

> *I do, Lord. I love you here. I love you in the place of Hope in my soul. I love you in this place of pain and anger. O Jesus, come into the heartache and the loss of hope. I love you here, Lord. I love you here.*

I know it might sound raw to love Christ in the very place of harm, but this we must do. For as we love Christ, it opens the soul to him. Harm of any kind causes us to pull away from Jesus (or our Father), like a sea anemone does when you touch it—it flinches, draws back, closes up. The soul does this with harm, rejection, disappointments. Going straight in and loving Jesus in these very places opens the door to his presence again. It also defeats Satan's purposes almost immediately.

Jesus continued, "Cleanse this place with my blood."

I do, Lord. I wash this place, all hope within me, with the Blood of Christ.

"Now cleanse it with the River of Life."

Yes, Lord, thank you. I cleanse hope in me with the River of Life. I cleanse all cynicism, anger, and despair. Thank you, Lord.

The pragmatist wants more practical explanation before entering into this exquisite mercy. *Where exactly is hope in me? But what about my feelings? How do I love Christ when I'm mad at him?* They might spend months processing all this, turning it over and over, and yet be in the exact same place of need—the need to give Jesus access. Yes, we often need the help of others to bring full and complete healing to our damaged souls. How blessed you are if you can talk things through with a therapist, priest, or prayer partner.

But I've had many clients over the years who could tell you all about their issues, using the sophisticated language of current psychology, yet they were no closer to their restoration. Clarity does not equate with healing; understanding does not equate with restoration. The Disciple of the Internet insists on clarity; the mystic says, *No—I need union with Christ here; that is my need.*

We need to get back into the refuge of God as quickly as we can.

Our Internet mind-set is often in the way of healing if the pragmatic materialist in us demands full understanding. Think about the people in your life—do you really understand everything about them? People are complicated, filled with contradictions and mystery; so are you. But still you love them and enjoy their company. You take trips together; you have rich conversations without everything needing to be sorted out. The mystic knows in their heart that they don't have to understand something in order to benefit from it.

> **THE DISCIPLE OF THE INTERNET INSISTS ON CLARITY; THE MYSTIC SAYS, NO—I NEED UNION WITH CHRIST HERE; THAT IS MY NEED.**

This is such a big idea, and so counter to our age of Internet Discipleship, I need to say it again: *You don't have to understand something in order to benefit from it.*

We don't have to dissect our experiences with God. We know with joy we simply invite him in, and follow him. The Revelation 3:20 invitation of Jesus is always at hand. The essentials look like this: We move straight toward the place of need within us. It might be fear; it might be a memory; it might be something we know needs healing, like hope. We move toward it, "enter" it, inhabit it.

In that place, we actively love Jesus.

I love you here, Lord. I love you here.

Now, this might take more than a moment. Linger there, loving Jesus, because as you do, you are opening your soul up to him. We invite Jesus in; we give him access.

Meet me here, Lord Jesus. I open this to you, Lord. Come. Come, Lord Jesus. Come.

Again, lingering helps; repeat those prayers.

Come, Lord. I pray for union with you here; restore our union here.

I find it helpful to play some worship in the background as I'm doing this, because it enables me to give fuller attention to the process. The human spirit is made to worship and responds eagerly to the opportunity. Your spirit will tune in to the worship, and God through it, and this pulls the rest of you along.

After I've lingered in these steps above, I wait and listen. Jesus is brilliant, kind, and creative. As your Creator he has access to everything in you and everything in your past. He will often say something you need to hear. He might ask a further question. As you grow accustomed to this type of communion, you will often see him inviting you to an encounter with him—perhaps to rest your head upon his shoulder, walk with him in a favorite place, or sit with him in a garden. As Thomas à Kempis reminds us,

> Turn, then, to God with all your heart . . . and you will see the kingdom of God come unto you. . . . Christ will come to you offering His consolation, if you prepare a fit dwelling for Him in your heart. . . .
>
> His visits with the inward man are frequent, His communion sweet and full of consolation, His peace great, and His intimacy wonderful indeed.[7]

Jesus and his entire Kingdom are yours, friends. Be a mystic.

I think if you practice this in your daily life with Jesus, you will find it easier to engage in the healing of actual fragmentation within you.

PAUSE

Take a deep breath.

What is stirring in you?

———o———

Every human soul is created for union with Jesus. The maturing mystic seeks union with Christ above any other experience. It is our essential homecoming on a daily basis.

I give everything I am to come into union with you, Jesus. I pray for union; I pray for oneness. Come, Lord—unite me with you in every way. Be the Integrating Center of my humanity.

But let's move on; the next chapter is the second part of this one. I'm hoping it clears everything up for you.

12.

Reintegration: The Healing
of Fragmented Parts

Let mine be a merry, all-receiving heart,
But make it a whole, with light in every part.

GEORGE MACDONALD

To be a human being is to be stained glass—beautiful in our bro-kenness, but a collection of many parts nonetheless. Someone once wrote, "You are every age you have ever been." They were speak-ing poetically but also naming something literal. You are six, eight, twelve, seventeen, and also your current age.

The human heart and soul were designed for Eden. We live far from it, far off in a war-torn world that assaults the soul from the moment we take our first breath. (Even beforehand; in the womb a child can experience rejection, fear, even abandonment as their mother feels and projects those things into the pregnancy.) Sometimes the harm we experience in this world fragments the heart. Parts of us break off and remain stuck at that particular age until Jesus comes to heal them.

We can call these areas of brokenness "young places" precisely because of the childish ways we respond when those areas are retraumatized. For example, someone gets mad at you, perhaps even yells at you. Part of you wants to run and hide in the closet—not the mature response of a forty-seven-year-old woman but that of a six-year-old girl. Or, the compulsion you have for ice cream whenever you are feeling anxious—not the mature reaction of a thirty-two-year-old man but rather the cry of a little boy who only ever felt loved when he was given ice cream. Most of us have had the experience, usually triggered by an upsetting event, where our internal world suddenly feels much younger than our current age. This is indication of the fragmentation caused by trauma, and let me add that when we are young it doesn't take massive trauma to fragment our heart.

Becoming aware of young places within you is a widely accepted practice in the therapeutic community. But our Creator foretold this centuries ago when the coming of his Messiah was announced in Isaiah 61:

> He has sent me to bind up the brokenhearted,
>> to proclaim freedom for the captives
>> and release from darkness for the prisoners. (verse 1)

The Hebrew for "brokenhearted" as used here is not a metaphor. It is blunt and vividly descriptive. *Leb* is Hebrew for "heart," and *shabar* the word for "broken." It is referring to a reality, not a poetic image. Elsewhere Isaiah uses *shabar* to describe a statue that has fallen to the ground and shattered into pieces. Actual fragmentation, not metaphor.

In the New Testament, James describes the divided human condition in this way:

If any of you lacks wisdom, you should ask God, who gives generously to all without finding fault, and it will be given to you. But when you ask, you must believe and not doubt, because the one who doubts is like a wave of the sea, blown and tossed by the wind. That person should not expect to receive anything from the Lord. Such a person is double-minded and unstable in all they do. (James 1:5–8)

The Greek here for "double-minded" is *dipsychos* (*psychos* being the word we get "psychology" from). *Dipsychos* means "split-souled" or "two-souled," vividly describing the fragmented human condition.

This will help you understand emotions that come out of nowhere, reactions to certain events that seem way out of proportion to the event itself. Inner fragmentation, the younger places within you, will help you understand certain compulsions, fears, and struggles that have not responded to the normal tools of discipleship or counseling.[1]

Nearly everyone has used the phrase "Well, part of me does, and part of me doesn't" to describe their inner dividedness over a family reunion, a risk they are being asked to take, even a simple invitation to hang out with friends. The phrase is far more accurate than most of its users realize.

Jesus chooses Isaiah 61 to announce his purpose in coming when he steps into the synagogue for his first public moment in Luke 4, placing the healing of our fragmentation at the epicenter of his mission to the human race. This is good news beyond our wildest hopes.

Remember now—Jesus is your Creator. He planned on you, fashioned you in your mother's womb, knows everything about you and everything about your story.

Jesus is also able to access hidden things within us, for he knows the depths and mysteries of our being. With his help, and the help of the Holy Spirit, we can locate our fragmented parts and give Jesus access to them for their restoration.

Let us proclaim loudly in this sad hour that Jesus Christ is the Integrating Center of the universe *and of our humanity*!

> **JESUS CHRIST IS THE INTEGRATING CENTER OF THE UNIVERSE *AND OF OUR HUMANITY*!**

Jesus Is the Center of All Healing Work

A few years ago, I spent five days and thousands of dollars to attend a trauma intensive for myself. As a counselor, it's not often that I get the opportunity to allow others to help me with my own damage. The week was facilitated by two beautifully gifted therapists, a married couple trained in trauma work. Our time together was utterly profound.

I rented an Airbnb for the intensive. After our first session, I left their offices and went to the rental for the evening. I arrived, carried my bags in, and began to unpack groceries. But I was feeling very uncomfortable in that house and I couldn't name why. Something about the place felt creepy . . . like a movie set where the unfolding scene isn't going to go well. I sat down in the living room to begin some of the homework the therapists asked me to do in advance of our second session. The discomfort in me grew. As I looked around, I realized that I was sitting in a replica of my childhood home. The broken lamp; the dingy furniture. It was unnerving, almost shocking. I went to the kitchen for a glass of water, trying to regulate my breathing.

The kitchen cabinets were eerily familiar; the *hinges and handles* on the cabinets caught my attention. I couldn't believe my eyes— they were the exact same design and age of those in my childhood home. I don't know why, but I hated those hinges. Standing there, stunned, there was no place to run. Some younger part of me was accessed; I began to weep profoundly, deep heaving sobs. The tears were partly from the trauma of my childhood, growing up in an alcoholic home, but they were also coming from a place of being *seen*, for I knew that moment was intimately orchestrated, right down to the hinges on the cabinets.

Jesus was moving in very quickly to access the young places within me.

I had to leave that house, though. I couldn't stay the week in that constantly raw environment. I prayed, *Jesus—can I leave now? Has your purpose here been fulfilled?*

Yes, he said. *Ask Joe.*

Joe is a friend who owns a few rental properties in that city. I called him and asked if he had anything available; he did, so I shifted locations. And Jesus kept coming.

The new house was on a noisy street, so I slept in the basement where it was quiet. When I woke in the night, in the basement, it reminded me of the fear that I had as a young boy sleeping in the basement of my grandparents' home. It even smelled the same, and suddenly that young boy in me was fully present. More tears, more access.

Once again Jesus was moving very deeply.

Each day as I came in for my next session, I would report to the therapists what had been happening. They marveled at how Jesus was accelerating things, preparing me for the work before us. "He is with us every step of the way!" they said. I share this story because it is essential that we keep Jesus at the epicenter of human healing.

An Unintended Quandary

The Christian community in the developed world—particularly in the West—has accidentally fallen into a model for the healing of trauma and fragmentation that requires wealth and access to experts. If you have thousands of dollars and if you can get to a trained professional, you can be healed.

But friends, what do we say to the fourteen-year-old girl being prostituted in India, Brazil, or in your own city—that Jesus cannot heal her broken heart unless she can get to a therapist? The captors hunt down those girls and kill them if they try to leave.

What do we say to the ten-year-old boy that is being delivered to motel rooms in Chiang Mai or Chicago to be raped by men every night? That Jesus cannot heal his ravaged soul unless he can get to a neurofeedback specialist?

Many valiant professionals are trying to bring these resources to the darkest places on earth. I salute them; I take my shoes off. But we cannot keep up with the need, and we cannot get to everyone on the planet. Are these broken children (and adults) left without hope? Without Christ? This is not the Gospel, friends—it's not even close.

Professional care is a gift from God. But for millions of children and adults, those professional resources will not be available in their lifetime. If we ignore the healing presence of Jesus Christ, available to every soul, we inadvertently back ourselves into a model that is exclusive and unjust, limiting healing to those with access to Western resources. No one wants this, especially not mental health professionals. They see the overwhelming need; they know something magnificent is required. The Gospel brings us hope when we remind ourselves that God has been healing human souls for thousands of years.

This is so important for our perspective that we'd better say it again: *God has been healing human souls for thousands of years.*

The healing presence of Jesus promised in Isaiah and Revelation (and the entire biblical story) is available to every human being on the planet—no matter where they live, no matter their situation. For the soul is healed through union with Christ, and he is available to everyone. That is the Gospel and nothing short of it will do.

Let's see if we can recover the Gospel of Jesus as it applies to human fragmentation in a model that any caring Christian community can bring to those around them.

Surfacing Younger "Parts"

We are all stained glass; we are all a collection of parts. There are younger places in every human being—it is unavoidable in this war. Those younger places surface at different times and in different ways. I want to assume the very best about Jesus Christ, so I am assuming that he is actively "surfacing" younger places within us.[i]

He might use distress in your inner life, perhaps triggered by circumstances. Emotions and reactions that come out of nowhere or which seem totally disproportionate to the situation at hand. Your compulsions and addictions are another way younger places could

---

i.　Some of you might be thinking Internal Family Systems; I will say more about that model later, but that is not what I am describing here. IFS is a way of describing internal "parts," or young places within us. But what I am laying out is far simpler and more universal. More on IFS later in the chapter.

be surfacing—the need for ice cream, video games, a profound long-ing to "go home," which you might experience as a desire to go back to your family home.

I remember the first time Jesus healed a younger place in my heart. This was many years ago; though I loved Jesus deeply and at times experienced his presence palpably, I had no concept of any-thing named in the past two chapters. I was a young mystic, and so I was not prepared for what was to happen—which shows that our loving Jesus is always, always coming for us.

One night I was awakened—either by something upset within me or by Jesus coming for that place. All I knew was that I found myself awake in the night, stirred by internal movements. I sat up, knowing whatever it was, it needed attention. With the covers still pulled around me, Stasi sleeping by my side, I sat in the darkness and allowed my restless heart permission to be present. I became aware of something that felt young within me; tears were coming. I felt lost and vulnerable, and I knew those feelings were not coming from adult me, but they felt very "true" nonetheless.

Now, it could have been provoked by something that happened the previous day; Jesus will do that. I know that as a young father and husband, I was feeling overwhelmed by the challenges in my adult life. I think some "younger me" was feeling it, too, but these younger parts do not have adult maturity and skills, so they can feel really overwhelmed (or rejected, abandoned—a whole range of strong emotions).

Mostly, I was aware that Jesus wanted me to be awake, and that he was simply coming for me.

All I knew to do at the time was not to push it away (we often push our younger parts away because they embarrass us or make us feel less in control). As I let my heart rise to the surface, I felt a boy of about six years of age in my heart, who simply needed attention. I prayed, *Jesus—come. Come here, Lord. Come to this place in me.*

I felt comfort immediately; I felt kindness. It's as if older me was now a bit to the side and younger me had Jesus' full attention.

What are you feeling? he asked.

I feel lonely. (I was often lonely as a child.)

May I come to you? Jesus asked with such tenderness it brought more tears.

Please, this younger part replied. *Yes.*

And that was it. I lingered there in *mystery*, sensing that for older me to insert myself into the process was clearly meddling and a bit arrogant; I also knew that trying to seize it in the moment to codify it or take hold was also wrong. I let Jesus be Lord. After a time I fell back asleep.

Over the years we have learned many more things about facilitating the integration of younger places (with much thanks to mental health researchers and professional clinicians). What I will lay out here can be used if you are facilitating healing for someone else, but it is equally applicable if you are seeking your own consolation with Christ in prayer.

Remember now—God has been healing human souls for thousands of years, way ahead of any latest advances in neurofeedback or psychotherapy. He is Creator, Redeemer, and Healer.

We can move with confidence into this, understanding that the soul is healed through union with Jesus. No matter the damage, no matter the story, the soul is healed through union with Christ.

NO MATTER THE DAMAGE, NO MATTER THE STORY, THE SOUL IS HEALED THROUGH UNION WITH CHRIST.

The next thing we understand and acknowledge is that Jesus Christ is able to access any part of your story, even those parts that you cannot. All of your days were written in his book before you lived one of them. Jesus Christ transcends time and space, and he is able to walk with you back into any memory and meet you there. He'll meet you there.

BEGIN WITH CONSECRATION.

I will typically start with a prayer of consecration like this (I will use the name "Jane" to personify someone I'm praying with, but again, you can do this for yourself too!):

> *Lord Jesus, you are our Healer. We belong to you, Lord; Jane belongs to you. We ask you to come. Come and surface the younger places you are wanting to minister to, Lord. We ask the Holy Spirit for his help. We command every foul spirit bound and gagged from this time and forbid any interference of any kind by the enemy and his forces. We ask the angels of the Living God to come and help us.*
>
> *Holy Spirit, let there be light. Help us to see and hear clearly now. Let there be light, Holy Spirit. Shine the light of heaven into Jane's inner being and into this healing process.*

ASK JESUS TO COME AND SURFACE THE PLACES HE IS WANTING TO HEAL.

Let's assume something has presented itself, for Jesus is eager to get to these places. It might be any of the many ways younger places surface that I mentioned above; something has caused Jane to ask for prayer. When you are doing this for yourself, go with what has presented in the moment if you can. This simple process can be very powerful when the distress is going on—the fear, compulsion, feeling "young" after a fight with your spouse or a bad day at work. Go with the moment if you can.

> *Lord Jesus, we ask you to come now and find the young places in Jane that you are wanting to heal today. Come, Lord Jesus, and find younger Jane.*

As facilitator, I am acting as a conduit for dialogue between Christ and Jane. (It is always easier to hear the voice of Jesus for someone else than it is for yourself, because you are not in the distress.)

It is paramount that you let Christ lead. Assume a posture of humility; do not simply bring your "tool box" to the process. You are both looking to Jesus and what he is doing.

I will always hear Jesus ask the person being ministered to, *Do I have your permission?* "Older Jane" needs to say yes.

GIVE THE YOUNGER PART A "VOICE."

This is important for them to feel safe to come forward, out of hiding. I will gently instruct the older Jane to "turn off the editor," that internal voice that wants to control everything. "You know the answers to most of these questions, but you need to allow the younger you to speak. Just be quiet; don't force anything, and don't make anything up. Give the younger you a voice. You are mostly just reporting what you hear and see. Let it unfold."

I will usually begin with the question, "Younger Jane, what are you feeling, sweetheart?" (I will use appropriate terms like "dear" and "sweetheart" to make them feel loved and safe. If that doesn't feel appropriate to the situation, you don't need to use such terms.)

If it is quiet inside, if older Jane doesn't hear anything, don't worry and *don't force the process*. Just assure younger Jane that she is safe. Take your time. "Little Jane, we want you to know you are safe here. You have a voice. What are you feeling, little Jane?"

Nine times out of ten, older Jane will begin to hear and even see some things. "I feel scared" or "I feel sad." Respond with kindness to what she says. "Of course you do. We understand." If things are still quiet, something is probably in the way. We will address this in the section on darkness below.

Sometimes I will ask, "How old are you?" If the session is taking place in a more formal counseling session where someone has been recounting part of their story, I will ask older Jane, "How young do you feel right now as you tell me this?" Either way, I am always also communing with Jesus through the process, and I will also quietly ask him in my heart, *How old are they, Lord?* Sometimes it helps to suggest, "Does seven feel true? I think I'm hearing she is seven."

Another question that might help—we are letting Christ lead, but this often proves true—is to ask young Jane, "Where are you?" The younger places are typically "stuck" in time and in a memory or place. I was working with a man in his fifties who experienced a traumatic event at fifteen. When we located the fifteen-year-old within, he was walking alone in the dark, on the same street as the accident, stuck there until Christ came.

Be a mystic, friends; don't get stuck in the mechanics.

It is common for the younger places to reply, "In my bedroom" or "In the closet," "Under the bed," "Outside in the tree house," or in the location where the trauma took place.

GET JESUS TO THE YOUNGER PART; ALLOW HIM TO COME.

One of *the* differences between inner healing prayer and counseling therapy is that in this process you are not taking time to go into the story at length. There may come a time for that—inner healing and conventional therapy go brilliantly together—but you need to understand that the enemy will do everything he can to thwart the coming of Jesus to the younger place, and distraction is often his tool. Don't get lost in the weeds.

I will ask, "Little Jane, can Jesus come and be with you?"

Again, children are mystics; they take to this process like ducks to water. The younger places in us are eager to have Jesus come, so let him come. Little Jane will typically say yes right away. If not, just linger for a moment, then ask the question again. "Can Jesus come and be with you where you are? Can he come alongside you?"

Eight times out of ten, the younger part will say yes rather quickly. If there is ambivalence in younger Jane, you might need to ask, "Do you know Jesus?" or "Does Jesus feel safe to you?" If they have been in abusive religious situations, you might need to work with the younger place a bit to assure them of Jesus' goodness. I will say, "Little Jane, that was not Jesus. He is mad at what happened to you. He is *mad* at those people. Jesus loves you; he is on your side!"

Typically with comfort and assurance, young Jane is then willing to let Jesus come to her, and often either they or you will "see" Jesus do just that—he will come into the bedroom, or wherever they are. This is gold; if Christ comes to the younger place, a marvelous and life-changing thing has happened.

We are not "imagining" a process with Jesus.

We are not suggesting scenarios.

Jesus is there; he is moving. Let him lead. I will ask younger Jane, "Is Jesus with you now? What is he saying?"

But there is more.

LEAVE THE HIDING PLACE WITH JESUS.

I've had many clients and friends come to a deep awareness of young places within them. They can name them; they have even "blessed" them. But that is *not* the same as integration. That falls short of the Isaiah 61 intentions of Jesus. He doesn't want us just managing a collection of parts in us. He wants to bring us to wholeheartedness, to integration. This usually involves a few more critical steps.

Often Jesus will ask younger Jane if he can take her out of the place of trauma—out of the closet, the bedroom, wherever you first found young Jane. I will assist in this by asking, "Jesus is inviting you to leave this place. Can you go with him? Is he holding out his hand?"

Young places are nearly always by this point eager, eager, eager to go with Jesus. We wait for them to say yes, and then Jesus will do it in an instant.

Sometimes Jesus will ask them, "Where would you like to go?" to allow little Jane to suggest a safer place, a special place. She might say, "To play outside!" or "To the beach!" And off they go.

Again, if things have gotten this far, it is marvelous. Little Jane is safe; she is with Jesus. Most healing models end here, but it's important *if Jesus is leading* to get to integration, to the "homecoming" of the younger part.

IT IS BEST TO GET TO INTEGRATION.

Younger parts that have been created through pain and trauma are not meant to remain broken off; they are meant to come back to the whole person, to be reintegrated. Let me share a few things we have found helpful in facilitating this.

I will ask little Jane, "Little Jane, how do you feel toward older you?" Because we can't get to integration if younger Jane is afraid of older Jane or if she has been experiencing older Jane pushing her away. Let younger Jane speak.

Quite often adult Jane will need to apologize for isolating younger Jane, or shaming her, or forcing her to "get with the program."

I will then ask adult Jane, "How do you feel toward younger you?" We need to get to the point that the adult can bless the younger part, to say things like, "I love you. You are an important part of me. I need you." This allows the young places to be willing to follow Jesus "home."

Then I will pray,

Jesus, bring this part into where you live in the center of Jane's being. We ask you to cleanse this precious part of Jane with your blood, Lord, and bring this young part home.

Oftentimes there are several "parts" ready for integration because they feel safe with Jesus, and so I will add,

Cleanse all fragmented parts of Jane who are ready to come home with your blood, Lord Jesus, and bring them home.

I might also have adult Jane say, "I welcome you home, six-year-old me. I welcome you back into my heart, precious little Jane."

What exactly is taking place during integration?

The best I can describe the exquisite mystery of this would be for you to picture an ice cube in a glass of water. The ice represents the broken part. It is the same substance as the water in the glass, but right now it is frozen and floating in separation. Integration and homecoming are when the ice melts back into the "host," the glass of water. There is no longer a separate part; they have become one again. This is experienced by the adult in many ways; initially, a peace will be felt inside which they have not felt for years. Then, over time, the reactions that were so out of place don't happen any more; the compulsions fade away because they aren't needed by the young part anymore.

The part becomes one with the whole because they were once part of the whole. This is deep and profound refuge, friends. Deep and profound.

Darkness

Notice that in Isaiah 61 the healing of fragmentation is directly linked to our victory against the forces of darkness (just like we saw in Psalm 91):

> He has sent me to bind up the brokenhearted,
>   to proclaim freedom for the captives
>   and release from darkness for the prisoners. (Isaiah 61:1)

Foul spirits are drawn to human suffering like sharks are drawn to blood in the water. Fragmentation is not a natural state of being as God designed humans; it gives a place for dark spirits to "land" or oppress humans. "Do not let the sun go down while you are still angry, and do not give the devil a foothold" (Ephesians 4:26–27).

Anger is not some unique and special sin; Paul is using it as an example that unresolved pain and emotion and our responses to them can give Satan a foothold. We have found over the years that healing of just about any kind—and especially healing fragmentation—often requires getting rid of foul spirits that are present. (This is why I include, in my opening prayer of consecration above, shutting down demonic interference.)

If the adult cannot see or hear anything going on, you might want to pause and ask, "Holy Spirit, are there foul spirits here interfering with the process? Let there be light, Lord; expose them and help us to banish them."

Also, once we do locate a young place, if they seem unable to speak or answer any questions, if they feel "held back," it may be because there are dark spirits trying to prevent their rescue.

I will turn again to the Holy Spirit: "Holy Spirit—are there foul spirits here interfering with the process? Let there be light, Lord; expose them. Who are we dealing with?"

God is faithful, and I or the client or someone helping in the time of prayer will hear from Jesus: "Fear is here" or "Death is here." We then order them to the judgment of the Lord Jesus Christ, never to return.

Sometimes ejecting the foul spirits is helped by the adult Jane forgiving her abusers. Now again—this is not therapy. In this critical moment we are not working through the trauma in the way a therapist might. This is hostage rescue; it must be treated like that. Move with tenacity to integration. The adult has the capacity to forgive before feelings of forgiveness manifest. When Jesus told us, "If you forgive other people when they sin against you, your heavenly Father will also forgive you," he didn't add, "after two years of thinking about it" (Matthew 6:14).

Then we call down judgment on the foul spirits.

I will add, "And every foul being that is in any way attached to this young part or inhabiting the fragmentation." Then we proceed with the beautiful healing process as laid out above, allowing Jesus to lead every step of the way.

We have seen Jesus come and integrate fragmentation so many times now, I could probably tell you one thousand stories if I had permission to tell them. These moments become for many people the most precious of their lives. As John of the Cross so beautifully wrote,

> How gently and lovingly you wake in my heart,
> Where in secret you dwell alone;
> And in your sweet breathing,
> Filled with good and glory,
> How tenderly You swell my heart with love.

Concerns

I know this process outlined above raises some questions, particularly in the mental health community. I'll try and address a few of those concerns here.

WHAT ABOUT CONVENTIONAL THERAPY?

I believe in therapy, neurofeedback, and all of the wonderful tools God has given humanity through professional training. These are gifts, and may they multiply in availability! It might be through therapy that the young places are discovered. Many therapists employ healing prayer as outlined above in their practices. In fact, I gave a young therapist interested in healing prayer an advance copy of this book. After a few weeks she wrote back to me:

> I felt invited to use integrative prayer with an older client I have
> been seeing for six months. I timidly asked if she would be open
> to prayer, inviting Jesus into a particularly traumatic memory we

have come to many times. She prayed for the first time in twenty years and invited Jesus in! He did more for her in ten minutes than I've done in twenty-five sessions. It was so incredible to witness the kindness and truths Jesus spoke to her! We've had several sessions since then, with lots of tears, healing, and Jesus showing up. It's truly incredible, and I am so excited to continue learning and using this with others as the opportunity arises.

WHAT ABOUT *PROCESS*?

Discipleship to Christ is something that plays out over time, absolutely. There are learned patterns in us that still need to be unlearned and replaced with holier patterns. Conventional therapy and good discipleship programs are needed in parallel with healing prayer to help folks into new ways of operating in the world. Healing prayer often brings breakthroughs we need to carry on in the process of maturity, but it does not replace what Eugene Petersen called our "long obedience in the same direction."[2]

BUT THAT'S TOO FAST!

Friends—the world is reeling in human suffering. Followers of Jesus are like medics on the field of battle. Many people and most situations do not provide lengthy and expensive options for human healing. Do we really want to say to Jesus Christ that he must live within the time frames we feel are appropriate?

ISN'T THIS TOO SIMPLISTIC?

It is simple, not simplistic. Adults want and need the world to be complicated; children do not. The young places within us are happy to meet Jesus and go with him. Children and mystics know that Jesus is wonderful, that he wants to heal us and lead us into refuge. Unless you become as little children, friends, you can never enter the Kingdom of God.

WHAT ABOUT IFS?

There is a modality that has become popular in recent years called Internal Family Systems, developed by Dr. Richard C. Schwartz. It's a model for understanding different "parts" of our personalities that play different roles in our lives. IFS has given therapists and their clients a language for talking about inner fragmentation. But we must keep in mind the goal is integration of those parts; Jesus offers *shalom*, wholeheartedness. Parts that are caused by trauma are not supposed to remain separate for the rest of your life in a system of parts that needs managing. Parts caused by trauma are not something to be managed or coordinated into an operating system. They need healing and integration.

The six-year-old Jane who was fragmented through the trauma of abuse is not a part to be managed for the rest of her life. That part needs to come home. She needs to be reintegrated, and Jesus is the best person in the world to invite into that process.

In Closing

The Christian therapeutic community in the developed world has unintentionally fallen into a model that essentially limits the healing of human trauma to those who have thousands of dollars, access to professionals, and years for process—thus excluding billions of hurting people around the globe. No one would say this is God's best for the world, especially mental health professionals who know the scope of the crisis.

Jesus Christ is the Creator of every person on this planet. He is also our Redeemer, shedding his own Blood for our rescue and redemption. He is also our Healer. While he blesses traditional therapeutic methods and the advances in neuroscience, he will not *limit himself* to the resources of the developed world to heal his lost sheep. To quote Athanasius again, "The renewal of creation has been wrought by the self-same Word Who made it in the beginning."

The soul is healed through union with Christ. In fact, to heal the soul *without* Jesus Christ is actually the process we ought to be calling into question. To help people to a better life without God is to help them *away* from God and into further independence from him.

Jesus is available to every person, anywhere on the planet, any time. *That* is the Gospel and it is truly good news.

PAUSE

Breathe.

Linger a moment.

I often find myself praying,

Lord Jesus—you are the Integrating Center of all things, including me. O Lord, pull all things back into you within me; reintegrate all things in me, Lord. Gather me up; hold me together.

Breathe again.

Jesus might be inviting you to go back and pray through something specific, using the process I laid out in the chapter for yourself.

Simply respond,

Yes, Lord—show me how. Take me there. Holy Spirit, guide this time of prayer.

13.

The Blood and the River

Now you have every spiritual gift you need as you
eagerly wait for the return of our Lord Jesus Christ.
He will keep you strong to the end so that
you will be free from all blame on the day
when our Lord Jesus Christ returns.
God will do this, for he is faithful to do what he
says, and he has invited you into partnership
with his Son, Jesus Christ our Lord.

SAINT PAUL, FIRST LETTER TO THE CORINTHIANS

We are ordinary mystics, growing and integrating into mature mystics so that we might lay hold of the provision of God in this hour—not just for ourselves but for those we love and minister to. The mystic Paul, speaking on behalf of God, promises us that we have everything we need.

You might pause a moment and ask yourself, *Is that what it feels like? Do I feel like I have everything I need to navigate this messed-up world?*

The joy of ordinary mysticism is that you come to *know* it to be true. Most people are waiting for God to do something remarkable in their lives. The mystic understands that all provision has been made; our job is to take hold of it. Then remarkable things *will* happen.

Paul goes on to say that the provision is there because we have been called to partnership with Jesus. Maturing mystics love this mind-set, this "partnership" way of approaching life. We learn all we can so we are fully prepared for all that Jesus has for us to do.

In these next three chapters, I'm going to give you a few more tools for the mystic navigating the war we find ourselves in and the trauma it produces. These are "amphibious" weapons and resources, for we draw upon them in the spiritual realm but bring them to bear in this besieged world.

To prepare you for where we are going, I want to equip you, beautiful mystic, with an understanding of *the use of . . .*

- The Blood of Christ and the River of Life
- The Fire and Glory of God
- The Breath of God

The Blood of Jesus

You might have wondered about the portion in my prayers when Jesus instructed me to cleanse damaged Hope in me with his Blood and with the River of Life. I meant it to catch your attention.

The Blood of Jesus Christ is probably the most sacred of all the treasures in the Kingdom of God, in heaven and on earth. It purchased our salvation, it cleanses us of sin, it breaks the powers of the enemy's hold on us. It sanctifies the soul, it cleanses memories, and it is a powerful weapon against the many poisons and toxins used by the kingdom of darkness against the saints.

> It has come at last—
> salvation and power
> and the Kingdom of our God,
> and the authority of his Christ.
> For the accuser of our brothers and sisters
> has been thrown down to earth—
> the one who accuses them
> before our God day and night.
> And they have defeated him by the blood of the Lamb
> and by their testimony.
> And they did not love their lives so much
> that they were afraid to die. (Revelation 12:10–11)

THE MYSTIC UNDERSTANDS THAT THE BLOOD OF JESUS IS A VERY REAL SUBSTANCE—AS REAL AS THE TABLE IN FRONT OF YOU, THE COFFEE CUP SITTING ON THE TABLE, AND THE COFFEE IN THE CUP.

This is the great anthem that goes up in heaven at the overthrow of Satan and his forces. It declares that we, the sons and daughters of God, overcome the evil one and his forces by the Blood of Jesus, the power of our testimony, and our refusal to fear death. I'd like to focus on the first of these, the Blood of the Lamb, for a moment.

The mystic understands that the Blood of Jesus is a very real substance— as real as the table in front of you, the coffee cup sitting on the table, and the coffee in the cup. We might not see it—it is part of the unseen realm now—but it exists, and we are urged to draw upon it in our need.

Is not the cup of thanksgiving for which we give thanks a *participation* in the blood of Christ? (1 Corinthians 10:16, emphasis added)

But if we walk in the light, as he is in the light, we have fellowship with one another, and the blood of Jesus, his Son, *purifies us* from all sin. (1 John 1:7, emphasis added)

I think you will find it very powerful to use the Blood of Christ to cleanse yourself when sin has taken hold, when your conscience cannot get free, when your imagination has been corrupted by something you've watched, or when some evil power seems to have come upon you.

Religion that God our Father accepts as pure and faultless is this: to look after orphans and widows in their distress and to keep oneself from being polluted by the world. (James 1:27)

The world defiles our humanity nearly every time we swim in it, like a rank swimming hole or a polluted beach. You will find it immensely refreshing and purifying to cleanse yourself with the Blood of the Lord Jesus on a regular basis—for example, after watching something that you feel "slimed" by, or passing through a dark part of town, an unholy shop, or a home where evil has been tolerated or welcomed.

Father, thank you for the Blood of Jesus. This precious, precious gift. I cleanse myself with the Blood of the Lord Jesus Christ now—my spirit, soul, and body; my heart, mind, and will. I cleanse my imagination. My gifting. I cleanse my sexuality with the Blood of the Lord Jesus Christ. Purify me, Lord.[i]

That "works" because the Blood of Jesus is a very real thing, and it purifies and cleanses us from every unholy thing.

I pray for the Blood of Jesus to cleanse every hotel room I enter (and rental homes and anywhere I find myself in the world). We have no idea what has taken place in those spaces, but we do know that sin defiles and opens the door for the enemy and his kingdom. If prostitution has been taking place there, for example, you will no doubt have dark, sexual dreams in that place . . . and probably similar urges. It can be disheartening, so cleanse those rooms!

Thank you for this hotel room [or rental, etc.]. I cleanse this room now with the Blood of the Lord Jesus Christ—everything in the physical realm, everything in the spiritual realm. I cleanse the objects and furnishings, the bed and bedding. I cleanse all media and the Internet here. I cleanse the atmosphere. I cleanse the ceilings, walls, floors, and everything in them with the Blood of the Lord Jesus Christ, and I ask you, Holy Spirit, to make this now a holy and sacred place while I stay here.

Here is another application. If you are having a difficult time with the "mystical life"—with regular experiences of the Trinity and

---

i.   You can, of course, ask Christ to cleanse you with his Blood if you are more comfortable. But let me point out that as we mature, Jesus entrusts us with more and more responsibility in our life with him. Spiritual warfare is a good example—he tells *us* to exercise this authority when *we* trample on snakes and scorpions. The young child waits for his father to tie his shoes for him, but the adult knows that the father trusts him to do so.

the Kingdom of God, the Blood of Christ can sometimes be the answer. If you are having trouble hearing the voice of God, the first place I would turn would be to cleanse your hearing with the Blood of Jesus:

> *Father, thank you for the Blood of Jesus. I cleanse myself with the Blood of the Lord Jesus Christ now—my spirit, soul, and body; my heart, mind, and will. I cleanse my spiritual hearing, Lord—the ability to hear your voice. May the Blood of Christ remove from me everything blocking my ability to hear you. Thank you, Lord.*

Everyone is created amphibious; everyone has a latent "prophetic" ability, the ability to operate within the Kingdom of God. If you would like to experience more of the Kingdom of God, try cleansing your prophetic gifting with the Blood of Christ:

> *Father—thank you for the Blood of Jesus. I cleanse my prophetic gifting, my ability to operate within the Kingdom of the heavens, with the Blood of the Lord Jesus Christ. Let everything that is blocking, harming, or preventing my ability to see and hear clearly the beauties of your great Kingdom be cleansed from me now with the Blood of the Lord Jesus. Holy Spirit, come now and refresh these faculties.*

The Blood of the Lord Jesus also breaks curses. Scripture takes blessing and cursing very seriously. From the Old Testament to the New, the people of God sought blessing and feared cursing because they knew that these are actual forces in the world, for good and evil. We know that Jesus Christ became a curse in our place: "Christ redeemed us from the curse of the law by becoming a curse for us, for it is written: 'Cursed is everyone who is hung on a pole'" (Galatians 3:13).

Paul is referring specifically to the curse everyone is under because of their own sin. Absolutely. But the Cross and Blood of Jesus triumph over other curses because his innocent Blood overcomes all cursing. We could get deeper into the weeds on this, but you don't need to in order to experience the benefits of it. The saints down through the ages have used this with great success; ask any missionary who has had to deal with shamanism or voodoo. The Blood of Jesus disarms all evil powers.

I had a curse on my heart for several years. I'm not sure where it came from (I have faced much witchcraft in my life), but I do know that my heart would sometimes hurt for no apparent reason. Twice I went to the ER because I was certain I was having a heart attack. They ran me through every possible test and said—both times—"Mr. Eldredge, we can't find a thing wrong with you. Your heart is strong as an ox."

Then I visited a mystic, a very ordinary man with an engineering background (who still used those 1950s pocket protectors in his dress shirts to carry pens). As soon as I walked into his office, he said, "Ouch! Do you know you have a curse on your heart?" His prophetic gifting allowed him to experience what I was experiencing. He broke the curse off my heart with the following prayer, and I haven't had another incident in thirty years. Thank you, Jesus! If you feel that someone has cursed you, or if you have been ministering or traveling in a place known for witchcraft and suddenly you are physically ill, I would pray this:

I bring the Blood of the Lord Jesus Christ against all curses that have been raised against me, either directly or by transfer and association. I cancel the power of all curses upon me with the Blood of the Lord Jesus Christ and in the authority of his mighty name. Let these curses and their effects be completely destroyed and removed from me now, by the Blood of the Lord Jesus Christ and in his name.

I've listed five examples here—can you see how rich the resources of the Kingdom of God are, how expansive?

The skeptic says, *Hmmm . . . maybe.*

The mystic says, *Wonderful! Thank you, God! I'll put this to use immediately!*

We celebrate and proclaim the Blood of Christ when we take the sacraments. I think it's interesting to note that some of the most serious disciples of Jesus would partake of the sacraments daily. C. S. Lewis took communion every day in the privacy of his room. Stasi and I have taken up this practice as part of our evening prayers nearly every night.

The River of Life

The River of Life is also an actual substance in the Kingdom of God, just as real as the Blood of Christ.

Ezekiel saw the River flowing from the throne of God in one of his greatest mystical experiences:

I saw water coming out from under the threshold of the temple toward the east (for the temple faced east). The water was coming down from under the south side of the temple, south of the altar. . . .

As the man went eastward with a measuring line in his hand, he measured off a thousand cubits and then led me through water that was ankle-deep. He measured off another thousand cubits and led me through water that was knee-deep. He measured off another thousand and led me through water that was up to the waist. He measured off another thousand, but now it was a river that I could not cross, because the water had risen and was deep enough to swim in—a river that no one could cross. He asked me, "Son of man, do you see this?" . . .

I saw a great number of trees on each side of the river. He said to me, "This water flows toward the eastern region and goes down into the Arabah, where it enters the Dead Sea. When it empties into the sea, the salty water there becomes fresh. Swarms of living creatures will live wherever the river flows. There will be large numbers of fish, because this water flows there and makes the salt water fresh; so where the river flows everything will live. (Ezekiel 47:1, 3–6, 7–9)

God did not show Ezekiel a make-believe river. If it wasn't real, he wouldn't have seen it. But he *did* see it, in great detail!

John the Beloved, also called John the Seer because of his authorship of the book of Revelation, was taken into the Kingdom of God by the Spirit. He visited the city of God, and there he saw the River:

Then the angel showed me the river of the water of life, as clear as crystal, flowing from the throne of God and of the Lamb down the middle of the great street of the city. On each side of the river stood the tree of life, bearing twelve crops of fruit, yielding its fruit every month. And the leaves of the tree are for the healing of the nations. (Revelation 22:1–2)

The City of God is a real thing, certainly; the Tree of Life is real; the River is real.

It is critical for the ordinary mystic to understand the availability of the River *in this current life*:

On the last and greatest day of the festival, Jesus stood and said in a loud voice, "Let anyone who is thirsty come to me and drink. Whoever believes in me, as Scripture has said, rivers of living water will flow from within them." (John 7:37–38)

It is an invitation as powerful as when Christ said, "If anyone opens the door, I will come in." Jesus comes, really; the River comes too.

We also have the wonderful promise of Psalm 1, which links our humanity to the Tree of Life planted by the River in the City of God:

That person is like a tree planted by streams of water,
   which yields its fruit in season
and whose leaf does not wither—
   whatever they do prospers. (Psalm 1:3)

A human life can only be evergreen if it is drawing upon the River of Life!

Invoking the River

Let us come back now to the traumatized human race.

Does the Church have anything unique to bring to the battle-field of human care? Are our resources only the same as those who do not know Christ? It cannot be! Jesus is the Creator, Redeemer, and Healer of humanity; surely he must have resources for us to bring to the injured in this hour!

We have found it immensely healing to cleanse body, soul, and spirit with the River of Life and the Blood of Jesus from all trauma and its effects. When you are ministering to someone, or when you are aware of trauma surfacing in your life—especially in the immediate aftermath of a traumatic event—you will find this sort of prayer immensely powerful:

> *We cleanse this trauma now with the Blood of the Lord Jesus Christ and with the River of Life. Every damaged part of our humanity [or "the humanity of Jane"]. We cleanse the body, soul, and spirit with the Blood of Jesus Christ from this specific trauma [name it]. We cleanse the body, soul, and spirit from the memory of the trauma as well. In the name of our Lord Jesus Christ.*

I'm not waving a magic wand here; there is often other work to do—either integrating prayer or trauma counseling. Of course. But in this war-torn world where injured victims are strewn across the battlefield, we can't wait to get someone into a program that might not even be available. God has made provision. The Blood and the River are very powerful substances for the cleansing and healing of trauma. This is especially true in the trauma of spiritual attack, which can be terrible. Washing it away works.

But then, all trauma is evil and often includes some form of spiritual attack, so this is very healing.

When I include "and the memory of it," I don't mean to imply some sort of heavenly "memory wipe." What happens is, while the memory remains, the "sting of death" is taken from it. We've found, for example, that we or those we minister to are able to sleep peacefully, untormented, after this type of cleansing prayer.

Really?

Now, I know, I know—for some of you, still Disciples of the Internet, this might sound like Santa's elves making toys at the North Pole, or fairy dust. Especially when dealing with something as heartbreaking as trauma.

But that is because you are a functioning materialist, trained to be so from the moment of birth.

You believe in your heart of hearts that the material world that you can touch, taste, and see is the *real* world. That everything spiritual is wispy at best, insubstantial, not real in the way that your clanking old Chevy is real. This is the fundamental crisis of the human soul, this functional materialism. It explains the near apostasy of the human race, the impotence of the Church, and it is the lie every mystic is desperately trying to break free from.

You don't taste, see, or feel oxygen, but it keeps you alive every moment.

You don't taste, see, or smell love, but it's the greatest thing in your life.

You don't see God (or rather, you don't see God *yet*).[ii] But are you really going to say that your refrigerator and your therapist are more real than God? More *helpful*?

So the other disciples told him, "We have seen the Lord!" But he

---

ii. Many mystics have seen and do see God. It's actually rather common.

said to them, "Unless I see the nail marks in his hands and put my finger where the nails were, and put my hand into his side, I will not believe." (John 20:25)

Recovering materialists and doubting Thomases, you are going to need to retrain your minds and your hearts and even your senses to the stark reality and unbreakable substance of the unseen realm, the kingdom of the heavens—which is simply the rest of reality.

C. S. Lewis was one of the most brilliant men of the twentieth century; he could talk you in circles through philosophy, ontology, and theology. He was a materialist who saw the utter bankruptcy of it and became a mystic. Lewis knew that the rest of the Kingdom of God is actually *more* substantive and *more* real than the world we think is the true stuff of reality. "Heaven is reality itself. All that is fully real is Heavenly. For all that can be shaken will be shaken and only the unshakeable remains."[1]

In his book *The Great Divorce*, Lewis attempts to shock his materialist readers into true reality by describing nature in the kingdom of heaven in this way:

It was the light, the grass, the trees that were different; made of some different substance, so much solider than things in our country. . . . I bent down and tried to pluck a daisy which was growing at my feet. The stalk wouldn't break. I tried to twist it, but it wouldn't twist. I tugged till the sweat stood out on my forehead. . . . There was a leaf—a young tender beech-leaf, lying in the grass beside it. I tried to pick the leaf up: my heart almost cracked with the effort . . . it was heavier than a sack of coal.[2]

God is real. His Blood is real. The River of Life is real. You can visit the River if you'd like, but I'll save that for a coming chapter!

PAUSE

Breathe.

Linger.

Pray,

Jesus—it's true. I am a functioning materialist, or at least parts of me still are. I know you are real; I know your kingdom is real. But I keep falling back into functional materialism. I'm a doubting Thomas, Lord. Deliver me from this lie! Deliver my heart and soul, my mind and strength from this unbelief I have been tutored into since childhood! O Jesus—impart to me the reality of the Kingdom! Give me the mind-set of the prophets, apostles, and mystics through the centuries!

14.

Fire and Glory

But the day of the Lord will come like a thief. The heavens will disappear with a roar; the elements will be destroyed by fire, and the earth and everything done in it will be laid bare.

SAINT PETER IN HIS SECOND EPISTLE

I was speaking at an important gathering in an evil city several years ago, so I asked my intercessors—the men and women mystics who pray for me—to rise up and help secure me in the refuge of God during the trip. Especially against "the terrors of night."

Sure enough, I woke in the wee hours that first night, in a strange room in a strange city, and that can be disorienting. As I struggled to come out of sleep and into conscious awareness, I was in that in-between state which many people report is where they are often able to hear from God. As I lay in bed, I could see images of firelight, or the shadows of firelight, flickering outside my window. I leapt up, thinking that the building might be in flames, but when I parted the curtains . . . it was simply night.

I closed the curtains and lay back down again, but as I looked through the sheer curtains, I saw the flickering firelight again and then I realized . . . I was being surrounded by the Fire of the Almighty, something one of my mature mystic friends had prayed for me.

The Things God Does

My friend's prayer for me came from the teaching of a "minor" Old Testament prophet (what a sad and mistaken appellation), less well known than Jeremiah and Ezekiel but equally mystic and remarkable in his ability to operate in the heavens and earth. Zechariah's visions are recorded in a short book bearing his name toward the end of the Old Testament portion of your Bible. I want to focus on one mighty, mighty promise found in chapter 2:

> Then I looked up, and there before me was a man with a measuring line in his hand. I asked, "Where are you going?"
>
> He answered me, "To measure Jerusalem, to find out how wide and how long it is."
>
> While the angel who was speaking to me was leaving, another angel came to meet him and said to him: "Run, tell that young man, 'Jerusalem will be a city without walls because of the great number of people and animals in it. And I myself will be a wall of fire around it,' declares the LORD, 'and I will be its glory within.'" (Zechariah 2:1–5)

God promises to be a wall of fire around his people, and within that shield, his Glory. Talk about refuge! Who could possibly assault us through the Fire and Glory of the Almighty?

I do think we should be careful as we claim promises from the Scriptures that are extrapolated from vague references, especially Old Testament references. Isaiah 45:2–3 would be a good example:

I will go before you
    and will level the mountains;
I will break down gates of bronze
    and cut through bars of iron.
I will give you hidden treasures,
    riches stored in secret places,
so that you may know that I am the LORD,
    the God of Israel, who summons you by name.

A wonderful promise, and one any son or daughter of the Most High would want to lay hold of!

But verse 1 makes it very clear that this promise was given to a specific individual at a specific moment in history: Cyrus, the last king of Anshan and founder of the Persian Empire.

This is what the LORD says to his anointed,
    to Cyrus, whose right hand I take hold of
to subdue nations before him
    and to strip kings of their armor,
to open doors before him
    so that gates will not be shut:
I will go before you.

Does this mean we are barred from laying hold of this promise in Isaiah 45:2–3? By no means! Despite the specific person and historical context in this passage, it reveals the *kinds* of things our God does. If we walk with humility, we, too, can ask God to do those kinds of things for us. The mystic reads and understands passages like this with a childlike heart and says, *This is my God! This is the kind of thing he does! I'm going to ask him to do it for me!* Our family and team have prayed Isaiah 45:2–3 into many circumstances needing breakthrough, with wonderful results. Humbly, with childlike faith.

Why would our loving God, who promises to be our refuge and shield, limit this beautiful promise from Zechariah 2:5 to a single moment in time? He's not like that, for the simple reason that his Fire and Glory are essential to his *nature*, his very being. So when we take refuge in him, Fire and Glory will of course surround us because *he* surrounds us!

> GOD PROMISES TO BE A WALL OF FIRE AROUND HIS PEOPLE, AND WITHIN THAT SHIELD, HIS GLORY. TALK ABOUT REFUGE!

Fire and Glory

In the chapter on taking refuge in love (chapter 10), we explored how our wonderful God—Father, Son, and Holy Spirit—is a consuming fire:

> Be careful not to forget the covenant of the LORD your God that he made with you; do not make for yourselves an idol in the form of anything the LORD your God has forbidden. For the LORD your God is a consuming fire, a jealous God. (Deuteronomy 4:23–24)

God's love is not merely *like* a consuming fire; it *is* a consuming fire. We saw how, many times in the Old Testament, when God comes down to rescue his people, the consuming fire devours their enemies:

> Clouds and thick darkness surround him;
>> righteousness and justice are the foundation of his throne.

> Fire goes before him
>> and consumes his foes on every side. (Psalm 97:2–3)

To be shielded with the Fire of the Almighty is a magnificent help!

Now, let's look into the Glory of God for a moment, the Glory that also protects us. "Glory" is a word that needs reclaiming, like "mystic." If you were to ask most church folk what is meant by the Glory of God, they would probably say it is the praise that is due to God or, if they are Bible-study types, they might say it is "the weightiness" of God.

Both are true; both are inadequate. How did Saint Paul see the Glory of God? Christ was raised from the dead through the glory of the Father (Romans 6:4).

A mighty, mighty power was at work to raise Jesus Christ bodily from the grave, whole and unconquerable forevermore. The preposition "through" is the Greek *dia*; it means "on account of, because of." Christ's resurrection from the dead was through and because of the glory of God; it displays the full power, beauty, worth, significance, and reputation of God, and it was the power, beauty, worth, significance, and reputation of God that did something so utterly unprecedented.

Glory.

The Glory of God is the full potency of God, the manifestation of his greatness, character, and power. The Glory of God is also his manifest Presence, for it was the Glory of God that filled the tabernacle and the temple:

> When Solomon finished praying, fire came down from heaven and consumed the burnt offering and the sacrifices, and the glory of the LORD filled the temple. The priests could not enter the temple

of the Lord because the glory of the LORD filled it. When all the Israelites saw the fire coming down and the glory of the LORD above the temple, they knelt on the pavement with their faces to the ground, and they worshiped and gave thanks to the LORD, saying,

> "He is good;
> > his love endures forever." (2 Chronicles 7:1–3)

What filled the temple? The manifest Presence of God. God himself; his potency. (Note that Fire accompanied it!) One more glimpse at this promise:

> Then the LORD will create over all of Mount Zion and over those who assemble there a cloud of smoke by day and a glow of flaming fire by night; over everything the glory will be a canopy. It will be a shelter and shade from the heat of the day, and a refuge and hiding place from the storm and rain. (Isaiah 4:5–6)

Here we have the Glory of God as a canopy, a place of shelter and refuge, a hiding place for his people! ("Hiding place" brings us all the way back to the forts children make.)

So when God promises to surround his beloved people with his Fire and Glory, that is incomparable refuge. Incomparable. A refuge we need in a war like the one we find ourselves in.

Invoke This!

Maturing mystics must call upon this. You have every spiritual gift you need; take hold of them. Invoke them!

We employ this in two ways; first, as shelter and protection:

Thus says the Lord our God: I will be a wall of Fire around you, and the Glory within. We call down your Fire and Glory, Father. Be the Fire around us tonight and the Glory within. Your Fire to shield us here in this home and your Glory to fill this place. Thank you, Lord!

Or we can invoke it as protection when we are out and about but feel a general sense of encroaching darkness:

I call down your Fire and Glory, Father. Surround me with your Fire and Glory, Lord. Thank you, God!

We also use it against the forces of darkness, as scripture so often portrays:

We call down Fire and Glory from the Lord God Almighty to consume our foes on every side. Fire and Glory, in the name of our Lord Jesus Christ, to consume the forces of darkness assaulting us.

I often need to do that after a rough night of attack, to make sure there aren't any lingering spirits still around (crush the serpent and scorpion):

I call down Fire and Glory from the Lord God Almighty to consume the forces of darkness that assaulted us in the night. Fire and Glory, in the name of our Lord Jesus Christ, to consume all forces of darkness from the night and set against us this day.

Try it. You'll see.

PAUSE

What are you thinking?

What are you feeling?

If it is anything short of joy and assurance, maybe you need to pray those prayers right now!

15.

The Breath of God

Then the Lord God fashioned the human, humus
from the soil, and blew into his nostrils the breath
of life, and the human became a living creature.

GENESIS 2:7 (ROBERT ALTER[1])

The Breath of God, the Breath of Life. This is how we came to be, how life was imparted to us by our Creator—he gave us his own breath. This essential relationship between Creator and created, the gift of breath given and received, is repeated throughout the Scriptures:

The Spirit of God hath made me, and the breath of the Almighty hath given me life. (Job 33:4 KJV)

O Lord, what a variety of things you have made!
In wisdom you have made them all.
The earth is full of your creatures. . . .
When you give them your breath, life is created,
and you renew the face of the earth. (Psalm 104:24, 30 NLT)

When the tragic human story plunged all humanity into death, God had a plan for our re-creation. He showed his friend Ezekiel, prophet and mystic, a vision about the coming re-creation of humanity, the new life that God would impart to those who come to Christ, who are indeed born again.

> The hand of the LORD was on me, and he brought me out by the Spirit of the LORD and set me in the middle of a valley; it was full of bones. He led me back and forth among them, and I saw a great many bones on the floor of the valley, bones that were very dry. He asked me, "Son of man, can these bones live?"
>
> I said, "Sovereign LORD, you alone know."
>
> Then he said to me, "Prophesy to these bones and say to them, 'Dry bones, hear the word of the LORD! This is what the Sovereign LORD says to these bones: I will make breath enter you, and you will come to life. I will attach tendons to you and make flesh come upon you and cover you with skin; I will put breath in you, and you will come to life. Then you will know that I am the LORD.'" (Ezekiel 37:1–6)

The breath of God creates us, and it *re-creates* us.

We should not be surprised then at the scene from the book of John, when the risen Christ breathed on his followers. After that beautiful story of Jesus coming to Mary Magdalene on Easter morn, later the same day he appeared to his closest disciples in the upper room:

> That Sunday evening the disciples were meeting behind locked doors because they were afraid of the Jewish leaders. Suddenly, Jesus was standing there among them! "Peace be with you," he said. As he spoke, he showed them the wounds in his hands and

his side. They were filled with joy when they saw the Lord! Again he said, "Peace be with you. As the Father has sent me, so I am sending you." Then he breathed on them and said, "Receive the Holy Spirit." (John 20:19–22 NLT)

I find it absolutely beautiful, poetic, and deeply apropos that when it comes to our re-creation in Christ, it happens through the Breath of God once again. Our Creator Jesus breathed on them once more.

There is a beautiful tradition in Hawaiian culture, dating back millennia, called *honi*, the "kiss of breath," where two individuals will touch foreheads or noses in order to exchange breath. "Native Hawaiians believe breath is the most vital life force, and *honi ihu* allows for the exchange of breath."[2] Just as God does with us.

You Narnian fans will draw immediate connections to the power of the breath of the Great Lion Aslan, C. S. Lewis's Christ figure, which restores, renews, and re-creates. In a scene much like Ezekiel's valley of dry bones vision, Aslan and the children come upon hundreds of precious Narnian creatures in the courtyard and castle of the White Witch—all of them turned to stone. Bereft of life, deprived of breath. Aslan breathes on them.

> **I FIND IT ABSOLUTELY BEAUTIFUL, POETIC, AND DEEPLY APROPOS THAT WHEN IT COMES TO OUR RE-CREATION IN CHRIST, IT HAPPENS THROUGH THE BREATH OF GOD ONCE AGAIN.**

Everywhere the statues were coming to life. The courtyard looked no longer like a museum; it looked more like a zoo. Creatures were running after Aslan and dancing round him till he was almost hidden in the crowd. Instead of all that deadly white the courtyard was now a blaze of colors; glossy chestnut sides of centaurs, indigo horns of unicorns, dazzling plumage of birds, reddy-brown of foxes, dogs and satyrs, yellow stockings and crimson hoods of dwarfs.... And instead of the deadly silence the whole place rang with the sound of happy roarings, brayings, yelpings, barkings, squealings, cooings, neighings, stampings, shouts, hurrahs, songs, and laughter.[3]

Like the morning of creation, or better still, the dawn of the first day of the New Earth. All through the breath of the Great Lion. Whenever I read this passage, I find myself saying, *I need this again, dear Father! I need you to breathe into me again, for I need your life afresh in me!*

> *Breath of God, Breath of Life, breathe into me again.*
> *Breath of God, Breath of Life, breathe into me again.*
> *Breathe into my heart and soul, my mind and strength.*
> *Breath of God, Breath of Life, breathe Hope into me.*
> *Breathe Love into me.*
> *Breathe Faith into me.*
> *Breath of Life.*
> *Breath of Life.*

Black Poison, Black Breath

I grew up in Los Angeles in the 1960s, back in the days before air quality management kicked in to get on top of the terrible smog in the LA basin. The topography there creates an inversion layer, which keeps all fumes and toxins pinned down in a dense blanket that sometimes looked like the smoke of a wildfire; there were days we couldn't see more than a quarter mile.

Summer vacation was the worst period for air pollution. I would come in after a day of romping so hard with my rambunctious boyhood friends—riding bikes, swimming, playing tag—that I could barely breathe. I could take only short, painful little sips of breath, my lungs had been so poisoned by the smog.

In this sad hour on the earth, air pollution has become the world's fourth-largest risk factor for early death. But if you live in cities like Delhi or Beijing, toxic air becomes nearly suffocating, bringing with it a host of ravages including cancer. Pregnant mothers exposed to these levels are likely to see premature birth, low birth weight in babies, and restricted fetal brain growth.[4]

Add to this the horrifying use of mustard gas in World War I and the Nazi gas chambers of World War II, and you begin to get a vivid picture of how the enemy wants to steal the very Breath of Life from us. After all, if God gives us the Breath of Life, we could expect his enemy to try and take it away.

When it is a *spiritual* attack, this goes way beyond air quality.

I don't know if J. R. R. Tolkien was fully aware of the prophetic nature of what he was writing, but it turned out that *The Lord of the Rings* was among the most important books of the twentieth century. It is a message for the Church in this hour, an epic parable of the last days and the last battles (with the final volume entitled *The Return of the King*!).[i]

> IF GOD GIVES US THE BREATH OF LIFE, WE COULD EXPECT HIS ENEMY TO TRY AND TAKE IT AWAY.

---

i. The books are far better than the films, by the way, if the films are your only acquaintance with this mighty work.

The Satan figure in Tolkien's Middle-earth is named Sauron. He has an elite team of dreaded demonic beings called the Nazgul. Their very presence is enough to cause valiant men to drop their weapons and cover their heads with cries of terror, so they are a good illustration of high-ranking foul spirits (as saints and mystics down through the ages will tell you). As the war for Middle-earth reaches its climax—centered around the siege of the White City called Minas Tirith—the Nazgul are released in force.

Casualties are brought into the Houses of Healing in the city, but the learned healers have no medicine to cure a terrible pall that hovers over some of the victims, a pall of death that would become known as the Black Breath. These poor folk fall deeper and deeper into darkness until the true king arrives and calls for a healing herb named athelas.

> When the black breath blows
> and death's shadow grows
> and all lights pass,
> come athelas! come athelas!
>   Life to the dying
> In the king's hand lying![5]

Stay with me now, because something just like this is taking place in the world. Our world. Right now.

Tolkien writes a prophecy into his story, whereby the true king of Middle-earth will be known when he arrives because he will be a healer. That king is Aragorn, and he comes to the Houses of Healing in the nick of time to save a valiant warrior:

Then he took Faramir's hand in his, and laid the other hand upon the sick man's brow. It was drenched with sweat; but Faramir did not move or make any sign, and seemed hardly to breathe. . . .

"[It is] the Black Breath," said Aragorn.[6]

The Black Breath, the enemy's most deadly weapon.

Aragorn asks for the herb athelas, but they have none in the Houses. They send an errand boy racing through the besieged city hoping to find some.

"The worst is now over. Stay and be comforted!" Then taking two leaves, he laid them on his hands and breathed on them, and then he crushed them, and straightway a living freshness filled the room, as if the air itself awoke and tingled, sparkling with joy. And then he cast the leaves into the bowls of steaming water that were brought to him, and at once all hearts were lightened. . . .

Suddenly Faramir stirred, and he opened his eyes, and he looked on Aragorn who bent over him; and a light of knowledge and love was kindled in his eyes, and he spoke softly. "My lord, you called me. I come. What does the king command?"

"Walk no more in the shadows, but awake!" said Aragorn.[7]

It is no coincidence that Aragorn breathes on the leaves, for he is the Christ figure, and *his* breath helps overcome the Black Breath.

Why do I bring this up?

We have watched a "deadly pestilence" roll through the world whereby devout followers of Jesus lose all faith in him overnight. Young people who for years loved and served Christ deconstruct their faith in a matter of months and are left holding nothing at all. Desolation and death suddenly appear in places where hope, joy, love, and life once reigned. It is like the Black Breath.

A friend of mine came under this sudden loss of faith; he called it "desolation." As a few close friends prayed for him, the Holy Spirit showed us a mental image of a black poison or tar-like substance on his heart. We removed it in prayer. The next morning he said this: "Guys, I haven't had a good dream since this assault began. God has felt distant. But last night, after we prayed, I had the most beautiful dream of me worshiping God and experiencing his presence!"

Such a beautiful breakthrough, in mystic fashion!

The apostle Paul tells us to "Hold up the shield of faith to stop the fiery arrows of the devil" (Ephesians 6:16). The "fiery darts" (*belē pepyrōmena* in Greek) Paul names here were the most advanced human weapons of his day, so he used them as an example of sophisticated demonic weaponry.[8] Had Paul written in this hour, he probably would have used imagery like "drones" and "GPS-guided missiles." Our enemy is a being of ancient intelligence and malice; he has many weapons, poisons, and technologies at his disposal. This Black Breath, or black poison, is one he is using globally.

But we have the Breath of God to call upon!

A Mighty Spiritual Weapon

I am happily situated within a loosely connected fellowship of mystics—friends of Jesus around the world who have developed a very deep life in him and honed their ability to observe with Jesus things taking place in the heavenly realms. Several of us were comparing notes this past year when we became aware of shared instructions we were each receiving from Jesus.

First, he had several of us—quite independently of one another—begin to invoke the Breath of God for our well-being, like I laid out above. *Breath of God, breathe new life in me.* We were delighted to learn that the others were hearing this from God too!

Next, Jesus began to instruct us to invoke the Breath of God as a spiritual weapon against these dark powers of the evil one—something clearly supported by scripture:

> With righteousness he will judge the needy,
> > with justice he will give decisions for the poor of
> > the earth.
> He will strike the earth with the rod of his mouth;
> > with the breath of his lips he will slay the wicked.
> > (Isaiah 11:4)

In the New Testament, Paul foretells that when Jesus returns, he will wipe out the remaining antichrist forces . . . with his breath! "Whom the Lord Jesus will overthrow with the breath of his mouth and destroy by the splendor of his coming" (2 Thessalonians 2:8).

One of my mystic friends just wrote to me this morning, saying that he'd been pressing into Jesus very deeply about the warfare in the world right now, and Jesus instructed him to pray the Breath of God against it. Further, Jesus took him to 2 Thessalonians 2:8. One hour later, I received an email from a *different* ally in *another* part of the world saying the same thing. A third friend had urged me earlier this year to use the Breath and Glory of God against all antichrist forces.

And yet again today, this email from another dear mystic:

> Well, I got attacked by the enemy last night. I woke up unable to take a deep breath. At first I thought it was my back from shoveling snow, but after I asked Papa he reminded me of a dream

I had earlier in the night where a giant had been slain and it fell across my body. I remember having to roll in my dream to keep it from falling on my head. Papa then reminded me to bring the Cross against it, which I did, as well as invoking his Breath of Life. It took several swings and a couple of hours to get out from under it. All this to say, thank you for bringing this "Breath of God" to us.

Jesus wants his people to understand and use this!

And so I encourage you to pray the Breath of Almighty God wherever you feel desolation, unbelief, or death trying to get in, for the Breath of God created us, and it *re-creates* us:

> *Breath of God, Breath of Life, breathe into me again.*
> *Breath of God, Breath of Life, breathe into me again.*
> *Breathe into my heart and soul, my mind and strength.*
> *Breath of God, Breath of Life, breathe Hope into me.*
> *Breathe Love into me.*
> *Breathe Faith into me.*
> *Breath of Life.*
> *Breath of Life.*

I would also use this mighty weapon against the warfare itself. Let's come back to Psalm 91:

> Surely he will save you
>> from the fowler's snare
>> and from the deadly pestilence.
> He will cover you with his feathers,
>> and under his wings you will find refuge;
>> his faithfulness will be your shield and rampart.

> You will not fear the terror of night,
>> nor the arrow that flies by day,
>> nor the pestilence that stalks in the darkness,
>>> nor the plague that destroys at midday. (verses 3–6)

Remember—the early church believed that "the deadly pestilence," "the pestilence that stalks in the darkness" referred to demonic powers and forces. I think this very pestilence is happening now; this Black Breath released against the entire human race—but especially against the friends of Jesus.

Let us command the Breath of God against this pestilence:

I command the Glory of God and the Breath of the Almighty against all desolation and death; all demonic pestilence; and all antichrist forces coming against me and my household. The Glory and Breath of God our Father and the Lord Jesus Christ to destroy all black poisons in every form from me and my household. The Glory and Breath of God our Father and the Lord Jesus Christ to fill our home and household, and to shield us from the forces of darkness. In Jesus' name.

This is mighty refuge, friends.

PAUSE

Breathe.

Linger a moment.

Let's pray once more for the Breath of God to fill us before we move on:

Breath of God, Breath of Life, breathe into me again.

Breath of God, Breath of Life, breathe into me again.

Breathe into my heart and soul, my mind and strength.

Breath of God, Breath of Life, breathe Hope into me.

Breathe Love into me.

Breathe Faith into me.

Breath of Life.

Breath of Life.

16.

Morning and Evening Prayer

Prayer is the place of refuge for every worry, a
foundation for cheerfulness, a source of constant
happiness, a protection against sadness.

SAINT JOHN OF CHRYSOSTOM

Despite their differences in time, location, gender, and culture, every mystic and saint down through the ages shared the same epicenter of their powerful life: prayer.

I do think the most practical and sustainable application of everything we've covered would be the habit of effective morning and evening prayer. I say *effective*, because quick little "Jesus be with us today" prayers don't do much except disappoint.

Ritual prayer—including written prayers like those I've shared throughout this book—are helpful in establishing a daily rhythm. They are helpful to make sure you cover the bases of essential prayer. And eventually you naturally memorize them, so you can pray them in times of duress when you don't know what else to pray.

Having said that, there is so much delight and power in

spontaneous prayers that are led by the Holy Spirit. I have quite an arsenal of prayer resources memorized in my heart, but I do not lean on them exclusively. I love to pause, listen, and then pray what the Holy Spirit is moving me to pray. Make room for that.

Morning prayer should successfully bring you and your household back into the refuge of God. Morning prayer should successfully accomplish these things:

- Bring you and your household back into the refuge of God.
- Restore your union, and align you with Father, Son, and Holy Spirit.
- Enable you to participate in the work of Christ on your behalf.
- Cleanse you and fill you with the Life of God.
- Shut down the attacks set against you.
- Enforce the Kingdom of God throughout your kingdom and domain.

I recommend morning prayer that accomplishes all of these things for the simple reason that any holes in these essential areas will leave you vulnerable in a dangerous world.

I've put a far more robust morning prayer in appendix 2. It is a much more thorough, much more mature, and much more effective prayer for those times when we need it. That version takes about twenty minutes. I recommend you give it a try every couple weeks and see what happens.

> MORNING PRAYER SHOULD SUCCESSFULLY BRING YOU AND YOUR HOUSEHOLD BACK INTO THE REFUGE OF GOD.

Morning Prayer

My dear Lord Jesus[i]—I come to you now to be restored in you, renewed in you, and to receive your Glory, Love, and Kingdom. I love you, Jesus. I love you, Lord. I take refuge in you. And I give myself to you completely—heart and soul, mind and strength, body temple, spirit. I cleanse myself with your Blood—heart and soul, mind and strength, body temple, spirit. I ask your Holy Spirit to restore me in you, restore our union, and fill this time of prayer. Restore our union, Lord. Restore our union.[ii]

Dearest God, holy and victorious Trinity, you alone are worthy of all of my love, my trust, and my devotion, and I give myself to you. You alone are life, and you have become my life. I renounce the Self-Life[iii] this morning, and I give to you, God, the place in my heart and soul, mind and strength, the place you truly deserve. Be first in everything. I ask your forgiveness for my every sin. Search me, know me, and reveal where we are working, Lord. Grant to me your healing, deliverance, holiness, and a deep, true repentance.

Heavenly Father,[iv] thank you for loving me and choosing me before you made the world. You are my true Father. I

---

i. I find it helpful to vary how I address Jesus to keep it fresh and intimate. I might say, "Beautiful Jesus," "Precious Jesus," or "Jesus, my very life."

ii. If you have immediate family (spouse and children), I would add, "In all that I now pray, I include my family. I bring them under your authority, I cleanse them with your Blood, and I ask your Holy Spirit to include them in this time of prayer."

iii. I use the phrase "Self-Life" to describe that sinful part of us that wants to drive the bus, get offended, indulge, make excuses for sin. It must be surrendered every day. More on this in chapter 17.

iv. Again, use the right words for "Father" that reflect your life with him. Sometimes I say "Papa" or "Abba."

love you, I worship you, and I give myself to you to be one with you as Jesus is one with you. Father—thank you for proving your love in Jesus Christ. I receive him and all his work you provided for me. Thank you for redeeming me in Christ, for re-creating me in him, and for making me whole and complete in him. Thank you for imparting your righteousness to me in Christ, for reinstating me in Christ at your right hand. I receive it all with thanks and give it total claim to my life.

Jesus, thank you for coming to ransom, restore, re-create, and reinstate me. I love you, Lord. I worship you. I receive again this morning all the work and triumph in your Cross. I take my place in the Cross today, dying with you to sin and the Self-Life, to Satan, to The World and its corruptions. I take up the Cross and crucify sin and the Self-Life.[v] *I bring the Cross, Blood, and sacrifice of the Lord Jesus over my life today, over my home and household. I cleanse myself with the Blood of Christ.*

And Jesus, I also sincerely receive you as my life. You are my life. I am saved by your life. I reign in life through your life. I receive all the triumph in your resurrection, and I take my place in your resurrection this morning. I enter your life, Jesus, and I receive your faith, hope, and love. I receive your wisdom, power, and strength. Your holiness. Your life in me. And I bring the resurrection and the River of Life over, around, and throughout my life today, my family, and my household.

Jesus, I also receive all the work and triumph in your

---

v.   You might find it helpful to be specific with your current struggles, as in, "I crucify all resentment" or "I crucify all lust."

*authority, ascension, and throne. All authority in the heav-
ens and on this earth has been given to you, Jesus. You are the
Integrating Center of all things. And I have been raised with
you in your authority. So I take my place in your authority and ascension now, and I bring all of my home, family,
and household under your rule and into your Kingdom.*[vi]
*I command the fullness of your Glory, Love, and Kingdom
throughout my kingdom and domain this day.*

*In the name of the Lord Jesus Christ, I now command the
Cross, Resurrection, and Ascension of Jesus Christ against
the forces of darkness attacking me and my household this
day—all foul spirits, foul powers, devices and technologies,
and all forms of black arts. Fire and Glory to destroy our enemies, in the name of the Lord Jesus Christ. The Breath and
Glory of Almighty God to sweep our enemies away before us.
I ask the heavenly host to carry out these orders now and to
rebuild the canopy of protection around my home.*[vii] *To guard
and protect us day and night. Your Fire around us, Father,
and your Glory within.*

*Holy Spirit, I love you. I need you. I worship you. I name
you Lord of everything I've named in my prayers this morning.
Come and reign, come and rule, come and fill, Holy Spirit. I
sanctify to you today the very fullness of my heart and soul,
mind and strength, body temple, spirit. Fill me afresh. Sanctify*

---

vi. You might want to be specific here with things that seem to be under attack or unpro-
tected, as in, "I bring our finances under your rule and into your kingdom." Or "I bring
our daughter's education under your rule and into your kingdom."

vii. Every Christian needs to pray a "canopy of protection" around their home. "He
stretches out the heavens like a canopy" (Psalm 40:22). We know the heavens surround
the earth like a sphere; this is much better than praying a "hedge," which is not a
360-degree sphere.

me through and through. Restore my union with Father and Jesus. Lead me in the truth today. Empower me in all things.

And finally, Lord Jesus, I put on the full combat gear of war, the full armor of God. I command the very fullness of your Glory, Love, and Kingdom throughout my kingdom and domain. Cloak me as I go forth today; hide me deep in Christ. I take refuge in you, Lord. All of this I pray in the name and authority of the Lord Jesus Christ, with all love and praise to you, Lord. Amen.

Evening Prayer

Most of you have spent your day out in The World, which, as we discovered, is *far* from a neutral place. The World erodes your union with Christ in many ways: the frantic pace, the barrage of media, the hatred and offense, all the corrupting influences. Every mystic knows the importance of evening prayer to return to the refuge of God and our intimacy with Christ.

Before I lay out the essentials of evening prayer, I want to explain one of the practices that is absolutely essential to finishing your day well, in union with Christ and safe in the refuge of God. That practice is Benevolent Detachment.[viii]

"[Cast] all your cares upon

> EVERY MYSTIC KNOWS THE IMPORTANCE OF EVENING PRAYER TO RETURN TO THE REFUGE OF GOD AND OUR INTIMACY WITH CHRIST.

---

viii. I devoted a chapter to this wonderful practice in a previous book called *Get Your Life Back: Everyday Practices for a World Gone Mad* (Nelson Books, 2020); I'd recommend reading that to enrich your understanding of Benevolent Detachment.

Him, for He cares for you" (1 Peter 5:7 NKJV). We are invited to lay down every burden and to give every person over to our Lord Jesus every day. You must untangle yourself from all the drama, the heartache, from all those temptations to give too much, say too much. Benevolent Detachment is how we do this, how we give over everything to God. The practice is "Benevolent," because it is not something done in anger or resentment; it's actually done in love. "Detachment," is referring to the healthy release that is essential to soul care, union with Christ, and mental health.

> Casting all your cares [all your anxieties, all your worries, and all your concerns, once and for all] on Him, for He cares about you [with deepest affection, and watches over you very carefully].
> (1 Peter 5:7 AMP)

Benevolent Detachment is expressed in this simple prayer: "I give everyone and everything to you, God. I give everyone and everything to you." We begin our evening prayers with this practice, and we linger there, releasing all things (often by name), so that we can return to union with Christ and the refuge of God.

Evening Prayer should successfully accomplish these things:

- Get you unentangled from The World.
- Bring you and your household back into the refuge of God.
- Restore your union with Father, Son, and Holy Spirit.
- Shut down the attacks set against you in the night.

If you do not accomplish these things in evening prayer, you won't sleep as well as you could. I want to add that Stasi's and my evening practices also include worship, Scripture reading, and communion. We will typically begin with one or several worship songs followed by listening to a psalm (often Psalm 91) read to us by an audio Bible program. Then we will go into evening prayer followed by communion.

As with morning prayer, I have included a more robust version of an evening prayer in appendix 3. But here are the basics:

> My dear Lord Jesus, I come to you now to be restored in you and renewed in you; I come to be restored in union with you, full and complete union. I take refuge in you, Lord. I take refuge in you![ix]
>
> I give everyone and everything to you now, Jesus— everyone and everything. I give you my family and all the people in my life. I give you my work. I give you the day behind me. I give you the future, Lord. I release the news. I release all things now in order to have you, Jesus, to come back to you in complete union and alignment.[x]
>
> I consecrate again to you my spirit, soul, and body; my heart, mind, and will. I consecrate to you all of my created being: mind and thoughts at every level of consciousness; my will and gifting; my emotions, heartaches, and all of my heart's life; my sleeping and dreaming. I bring the cleansing Blood of the Lord Jesus over, around, through, and throughout all of me and all of our union.
>
> Holy Spirit, restore me, renew me, fill me; restore my union with Jesus and Papa, and lead this time of prayer. In all

---

ix. If you are praying with your spouse or children, you will want to say "we" instead of "I."

x. We find it helpful to name the things that we are caught up in. You might also pray, "What do I need to release, Lord?"

that I now pray, I stand in utter agreement with you, Jesus, and with everyone praying for me in heaven and on earth.[xi]

Holy Spirit, help me to ascend. I ascend in my heart and I ascend in the heavens, Lord Jesus, and I bring all things of my home and household, my kingdom and domain, under your rule and into your Kingdom.[xii] *I bring all things of my sleep and dreaming under your rule and into your refuge tonight.*[xiii]

I now call down Fire and Glory and the Breath of Almighty God to destroy every form of foul and unclean spirit coming against me and my household this night. Full and final judgment in the name of the Lord Jesus Christ against the forces of darkness that have been attacking me this day, and all who are arrayed against me and my household tonight.[xiv]

I also command the body and Blood of the Lord Jesus Christ, Fire and Glory, and the Breath of Almighty God to destroy every form of foul power, witchcraft, and black art raised against me and my household. Destroy immediately every curse, spell, ritual, and sacrifice; all forms of black arts and their technologies that have been sent against me and my

---

xi. Without getting into theological debate, we know for certain that Jesus makes intercession for us in heaven (Romans 8:34). Many traditions also believe that the saints are interceding for us.

xii. If you live in an apartment, say "apartment." If you have a room in a house or apartment, bring your room under the jurisdiction of Jesus.

xiii. Ephesians 2:6 makes it clear that you have been seated with Christ at the right hand of the Father. Prayers of authority, jurisdiction, and spiritual warfare are much more effective when issued from that place of authority, so I intentionally "ascend" there because I am invited to.

xiv. You might pause here and ask Jesus what enemies you need to deal with directly, as in, "All foul spirits of fear, all hatred and death . . ."

household; along with every empowering spirit all the way back to their origins, in the name of the Lord Jesus Christ.

I command the Fire and Glory and the Blood of the Lord Jesus Christ between me and my household and The World tonight.

I command the Kingdom of God and the majesty of the Lord Jesus Christ between me and the kingdoms of this world, including this local kingdom where I live.[xv]

Lord Jesus, I command the fullness of your love and your Kingdom, your Blood and your Glory, between me and my household and all people tonight—their spirit, soul, and body, their sin and warfare. This includes all family, friends, neighbors, coworkers—every person. Only the love of the Lord Jesus Christ between us!

I summon now the heavenly host, the angels and heavenly beings that are sent to help me in the name of the Lord Jesus Christ. With love, honor, and blessing I ask for their help in everything. Let every order be carried out. Let the canopy around my home be rebuilt, cleansed, and sealed again with the Blood of Jesus.

Holy Spirit, I ask you to fill my home and household, my sleeping and night.

I command all of this in the name of the Lord Jesus Christ, with all glory and praise to him. Thank you, Lord!

This is the practical expression of our active participation in the

---

xv. I am referring to the city and region you live in, which is under the control of local foul spirits (for the biblical background to this claim, see, for example, 1 John 5:19 and Daniel 10:12–13). It is very helpful to keep Christ between you and the kingdoms of this world, because they are not neutral ground!

refuge of Psalm 91 as mature friends of God. It will immensely help you and those who live under your roof. We are ordinary mystics growing into maturing mystics. It's completely normal if things feel a little bumpy right now. Hang in there; you'll get this.

Morning and evening prayer (maybe *especially* evening prayer) have another holy gift that the saints and mystics through the ages talk quite a lot about: They have a sanctifying effect upon the soul because we often don't *feel* like praying. Far too often it feels like a hassle to me, especially at the end of a rough day. I just want to eat a bowl of cereal and go to bed. But it is on those nights, after rough days, that I most need evening prayer, and when I choose against my feelings to go ahead and pray the entire prayer with focus and attention, it sanctifies my soul.

And I really do want my soul sanctified.

PAUSE

Breathe.

What are you feeling?

What are your current morning and evening rituals?

You might be thinking, *This is level-one prayer!?* Yes. The practice of serious prayer has been lost to the Church in this frantic hour. This only takes about ten minutes, friends. It will develop your soul in wonderful ways.

17.

What Can I Expect?

His visits with the inner man are frequent.

THOMAS Á KEMPIS

We began our search looking for refuge because I am convinced this is the urgent need of the hour. You will find yourself helping others into the shelter of God in the days ahead; let's get everyone into the shelter of the Most High!

And . . . there is so much more that the ordinary mystic becoming a mature mystic gets to experience!

I confessed in chapter 2 that I was taking an enormous risk by using the word *mystic* to explain and invite my readers into the normal Christian life. The word has been widely misused and misinterpreted, and critics could dismiss and damn this book without reading it.

I'm going to take an even greater risk now in order to open up to you possibilities with God and his magnificent Kingdom. I do this in love because we need what the old saints would call "succor" and "consolation." We need the deep ministry of Jesus, facilitated through Kingdom experiences. Sometimes one simple word spoken to us from Christ in an intimate moment can carry us through enormous loss or suffering.

If you take a frog, a true amphibian, and you keep it in only water, it will die. If you keep it on only dry land, it will die. It needs both habitats to flourish. So do we. Man does not live by bread alone. We need the nourishment of God and his full Kingdom in order to flourish—especially in an hour like this one. That is why I am going to share the following possibilities.

> **WE NEED THE NOURISHMENT OF GOD AND HIS FULL KINGDOM IN ORDER TO FLOURISH—ESPECIALLY IN AN HOUR LIKE THIS ONE.**

This is not for curiosity and never for boasting. Never for comparison of one spiritual life to another. This is sustenance, strength, guidance, healing. It is succor and consolation for the friends of Jesus.

Assurance

Julian of Norwich is one of the better-known mystics, and rightly so. As an anchorite, someone who lived in solitude, her life was utterly and completely given over to Christ. Julian is remembered for her humility, holiness, and tender compassion for the human race. C. S. Lewis admired her greatly and often quoted her. She lived in the fourteenth and fifteenth centuries and is best known for her work *Revelations of Divine Love*, the record of a series of sixteen conversations she had with Jesus when she was near death (remarkably, afterward she lived more than forty additional years!).

Julian had been plagued all her life with a question that has deeply troubled many tender souls: Why did God allow sin to take place, knowing how awful the consequences would be?

> In my folly, before this time I often wondered why, by the great foreseeing wisdom of God, the onset of sin was not prevented: for then, I thought, all should have been well. This impulse [of thought] was much to be avoided, but nevertheless I mourned and sorrowed because of it, without reason and discretion.
>
> But Jesus, who in this vision informed me of all that is needed by me, answered with these words and said: "It was necessary that there should be sin; but all shall be well, and all shall be well, and all manner of things shall be well."[1]

All shall be well, and all shall be well, and all manner of things shall be well. These words have comforted Jesus-followers for centuries. My body relaxes even as I type them here. They are essential consolation. At the Restoration of All Things this promise will make perfect sense to us; in this we can fully trust, like a child.

This sort of intimate assurance given by revelation is the kind of thing God does; this consolation he still offers to ordinary mystics.

I have friends whose hearts were broken when their son walked away from Jesus. Hours of prayer and intercession over years have not—yet—seen him return to God. Once, when they were grieving as only parents can grieve, they turned to prayer, silently communing with Jesus. Suddenly, without conversing with each other and at the same moment, Jesus said to each of them individually, "Look."

When Jesus says, "Look," mystics understand he often wants to show them something. It might be a glimpse at things from heaven's point of view or it might be a glimpse into future events yet to unfold.

They were both in prayer, still silent, yet they each saw their son in the Kingdom of God, after the Restoration of All Things. He was 100 percent himself, as he had never been himself. He was laughing. He was well. He was with one of his children. He obviously fit in the Kingdom. He was *home*. They shared what they had been shown, with the sweet confirmation that the other had been shown the exact same thing. And because they are mystics, that was all they needed. Whatever the story looks like now, their son will be there. All shall be well.

These gifts from the Lord Jesus can be so healing. Many times over the years Jesus has shown me pictures, or visions, or glimpses into the New Earth (it's everything you hoped for, friends). The sheer beauty of it was consolation, promise, assurance.

You can come to Jesus in every need of assurance, and he *will* speak to you.

Conversational Intimacy

From Julian to Dallas Willard, the writings of the mystics down through the ages are filled with records of conversations they had with the Lord Jesus. None of them report the fact that they are hearing from Jesus (or Papa or Holy Spirit) as unusual at all.

Because it is not unusual.

As Brother Lawrence assured us, "There is not in the world a kind of life more sweet and delightful, than that of a continual conversation with God; those only can comprehend it who practice and experience it."[2]

The late Dallas Willard felt this was so essential to the Christian life that he wrote his first book on the practice: *Hearing God:*

Developing a Conversational Relationship with God. In this book he tells many stories from his own life and those of the saints he knew. The revelations of love Julian received came through conversation with Jesus. There is, of course, the famous story that got Saint Francis underway, as Saint Bonaventure reported:

> For on a certain day, when he had gone forth to meditate in the fields, he was walking nigh the church of Saint Damian, which from its exceeding great age was threatening to fall, and, at the prompting of the Spirit, went within to pray. Prostrating himself before an Image of the Crucified, he was filled with no small consolation of spirit as he prayed. And as with eyes full of tears he gazed upon the Lord's Cross, he heard with his bodily ears a Voice proceeding from that Cross, saying thrice: "Francis, go and repair My House, which, as thou seest, is falling utterly into ruin."[3]

Francis began taking stones to rebuild that chapel; in years to come he was to realize that God meant *the* Church, and of course dear Francis had a sweeping, global influence on the renewal of the body of Christ.

Conversation with Jesus carries right on into the present moment.

The father of a dear woman and mature mystic I know was dying; but he was hospitalized in a different state. She had made visits, as so many of you have, but as happens to adult children in this situation, she could not stay through weeks and weeks of uncertainty; she needed to return home. Her sister remained there with him, which was some consolation. But my friend could not.

In the middle of the night, Jesus woke her from sleep and said to her, *Your phone is ringing.*

She knows the voice of Jesus, so she rose, went out to the kitchen, and sure enough—her phone was ringing. It was her sister calling to patch her into her father's hospital room so she could say goodbye right before he passed.

Learning to recognize the voice of God is something we learn and grow into over a lifetime. But we are trying to be frank and realistic about our situation in the world, and so this needs to be said as clearly and honestly as can be:

Hearing the voice of God is essential to Christian discipleship.

It is not optional.

It is not for a select few.

For one thing, Scripture teaches it on nearly every page, whether by the example of saints past or by direct command to all who believe.

What would we think of a father or mother who never spoke to their children? Imagine that these parents provided for their children's needs and spent time with them but never spoke a word to them. We would call it child abuse, neglect, or abandonment. It would be terribly traumatizing. Nor would we be satisfied with an occasional word; we would insist that the relationship involve regular, intimate communication. The same would be true for any marriage, any friendship. How could you call someone your friend if they met you for coffee and spent an hour with you but never spoke a word? Never asked you how you were doing? Never laughed together over shared stories?

Friends, we are created in the image of a highly relational Being, a God who is triune in relationship! That is why we are highly relational beings ourselves. It is absurd and blasphemous to accept a theology that makes hearing the voice of God exceptional or occasional.

The gatekeeper opens the gate for him, and the sheep listen to his voice. He calls his own sheep by name and leads them out. When he has brought out all his own, he goes on ahead of them, and his sheep follow him because they know his voice. But they will never follow a stranger; in fact, they will run away from him because they do not recognize a stranger's voice. (John 10:3–5)

If this isn't central to the scriptural witness, nothing is.

I'm saying this with great emphasis because I know too many dear, dear lovers of God who have, for one reason or another, written this off for themselves. Sometimes because they found it difficult to learn the practice and concluded it wasn't for them. Or perhaps more frequently because they saw it abused by others and withdrew from it. Or because their spiritual leaders told them it isn't available, which is of course poor theology and completely detached from reality.

Let no one steal this from you, friends. It is too essential in an hour like this one.

Joy

Over years of reading the saints or their biographers, I've been delighted to discover a recurring thread throughout these records of Christian mysticism: the profound experience of joy from God. Of course, there is David, who says deliciously inviting things like, "You will fill me with joy in your presence" (Psalm 16:11). It makes my heart say, *Really? I want to experience that, Lord!* C. S. Lewis entitled his autobiography *Surprised by Joy.* Here is another example, from John Wesley's life:

On another occasion, [John] Wesley and his brother Charles took a walk in a meadow intending to sing psalms in praise to God. Just as they started to sing Charles burst into loud laughter. Before long, John too was laughing uncontrollably. "Nor could we possibly refrain, though we were ready to tear ourselves in pieces, but we were forced to go home without singing another line."[4]

Pascal said that his conversion was filled with "Joy, joy, joy, tears of joy."[5] Methodist leader John Walsh wrote, "The influence of His Spirit wrought so powerfully upon me, that my joy was beyond expression."[6] And there is a sweet, sweet story of the joy that came to Augustine's mother when he finally came as an adult to tell her of his dramatic conversion to Christ:

> Then we went in to my mother, and told her what happened, to her great joy. We explained to her how it had occurred—and she leaped for joy triumphant; and she blessed thee, who art "able to do exceedingly abundantly above all that we ask or think." For she saw that thou hadst granted her far more than she had ever asked for in all her pitiful and doleful lamentations. For thou didst so convert me to thee that I sought neither a wife nor any other of this world's hopes, but set my feet on that rule of faith which so many years before thou hadst showed her in her dream about me. And so thou didst turn her grief into gladness more plentiful than she had ventured to desire.[7]

(Did you notice that God had given Augustine's mother a vision in a dream about his later conversion?)

After an inner healing session, a friend of mine said, "I walked around for the next two hours with a smile I couldn't get off my face.

I was just smiling and smiling at the joy of the relief, the intimacy and the healing I had experienced."

During times of exceptionally difficult spiritual warfare, God will often say to me, *Turn into my joy.* By which I know he means, *Drop into your heart and commune with me. Once there, turn into my joy. Enter it. Inhabit it. Let it inhabit you.*

And oh, what a difference it makes.

Guidance

"What should I do, Lord?" is probably one of the most-often prayed prayers on the planet. "What should I do with this situation?" and "What should I do with my life?"

The ordinary mystic is far better situated to receive answers to those questions than the person living at some distance from God. Learning to hear the voice of God will be the primary means. My fellowship of mystics could tell a hundred thousand stories at this point of receiving guidance great and small.

But God often uses other creative avenues, including dreams, visions, and encounters. I mentioned Luther as a mystic earlier; here is an example:

Luther's own spiritual journey involved experiences with the living God. Late in life he described his (oft-debated) "tower experience": "All at once I felt that I had been born again and entered into paradise itself through open gates. Immediately I saw the whole of Scripture in a different light." In language that recalls Paul's vision of the third heaven (2 Cor 12:1–4), Luther's experience [*Erfahrung*] of the nearness and in-breaking of God utilizes mystical language; it was nearly inexpressible and was facilitated as much through the heart as through the mind.[8]

You'll remember that Joseph the son of Jacob was given a very important dream from God when he was still a lad. Saint John Bosco received a calling upon his life in a dream when he was also a boy, a vision that would blossom into a global ministry to children through schools and orphanages:

> When John was nine years old, he had a dream that was so clear it felt like real life. He was standing in a field full of very poor boys who were acting up, fighting, playing, and saying awful things about God. John was a poor boy, just like them. But he shouted at them to get them to stop. When he did, a man with a glowing face appeared, wearing a white robe.
>
> "You will have to win these friends of yours with kindness," the man said, "not with blows. Show them that sin is ugly and goodness is beautiful."
>
> John was scared and confused. "I'm just a boy," he said. "How can you order me to do something that's impossible?"
>
> "I'll send you a teacher," the man told him.
>
> Then a woman appeared, who glowed as if she were covered in stars, and the children around John turned into wild animals.
>
> "Stay in your field for now," the woman told him. "This is where you'll learn to be humble and strong."
>
> When she said this, all the wild animals turned into lambs. "Everything will be clear in time," the woman told John.[9]

Many years ago, when we were starting our ministry, we received a number of words from Jesus about a "Center" we would create for discipleship. Like many people, we then brought *our own assumptions* to those promises; we assumed Jesus meant that we would build an actual Center, a monastic retreat of sorts. We were on the verge of buying property when I had a dream where God made it clear to me that the Center would not happen in that way. I woke dejected because we had brought our assumptions into the story. But as time unfolded, we realized the utter relief of not having to maintain a facility. Our work has spread all over the world in many "Centers," and for that we are immensely grateful. Jesus rescued us through that dream.

And right now, across the globe, Jesus is showing up in the lives of thousands of Muslims, bringing them to salvation by introducing himself to them in their dreams. I commend to you the book *A Wind in the House of Islam* for hundreds of these beautiful, encouraging stories. Here is one example:

A colleague has been serving God among Muslims long enough to have heard countless testimonies of dreams in which a "being who shone bright as light" appeared to them, beckoning them to come to him. In a recent encounter with a Muslim man who had experienced such a dream, my colleague simply opened his Bible to the story of Christ's transfiguration in Matthew 17 and invited his Muslim friend to read the first two verses: "After six days Jesus took with him Peter, James and John the brother of James, and led them up a high mountain by themselves. There he was transfigured before them. *His face shone like the sun, and his clothes became as white as the light*" (Matthew 17:1–2, emphasis added)." Startled by the discovery, the Muslim responded, "That's the guy, the guy in my dreams! Who is this?"[10]

Isn't Jesus wonderful?!

Speaking of wonderful, let's turn to the central treasure of the mystic life.

Communion

Jesus Christ dwells deep in the heart of every person who invites him to. From that point forward he can be found deep within, and learning to commune with Jesus in your heart is the greatest treasure on this side of his return. As Jeanne Guyon instructed,

> Therefore, from the very beginning you find great joy in knowing that your Lord is within you and that you can find him and enjoy him in your inmost being. . . . When you are thus turned toward God, you find it easy to return there again and again. The longer you continue to turn inward to God, the nearer you are drawn to him and the more firmly you adhere to him.
>
> By moving into that inmost sanctuary again and again, it becomes natural, even habitual to live in the presence of God.[11]

Teresa of Avila spoke of the "garden of your heart," a little Eden within where we go to meet with Jesus:

> The beginner must realize that in order to give delight to the Lord he is starting to cultivate a garden: . . . Then He will often come to take delight in this garden and find His joy among these virtues.[12]

This is the daily practice of a lovely mystic I know. She has a special room in her house devoted only to worship and prayer and communing with Jesus. She will go into that room, turn inward, and "drop into" the garden of her heart. There she is able to receive many things from Jesus: "Often we will just sit together, our backs against a tree. Just to be in his presence is everything. Sometimes he will take me to The River of Life and I will get in and just soak in the healing presence of his Life washing over me."

Inner communion with Jesus provides so many things to his followers: consolation, healing, rejuvenation, peace, loads of playful encounters—I could go on and on. Learning this practice is so wonderful that I will add to appendix 1 some guidance into what I call the Prayer of Descent, which is learning to drop into your innermost being and find Jesus there.

> INNER COMMUNION WITH JESUS PROVIDES SO MANY THINGS TO HIS FOLLOWERS: CONSOLATION, HEALING, REJUVENATION, PEACE, LOADS OF PLAYFUL ENCOUNTERS.

Remember, we are progressing from ordinary mystics to mature mystics over time. If all you initially experience is a sense of his love or peace, that's wonderful! It's so nourishing, so reassuring.

Inner Healing

The earlier chapters on integration (chapters 11 and 12) assume the active presence of Jesus working deep within us, as Revelation 3:20 promises: "If you hear my voice and open the door, I will come in, and we will share a meal together as friends" (NLT).

So many breathtaking stories have come from the practice of inner healing prayer.

Friends were leading a woman through integration prayer—which at its simplest is Jesus coming to the wounded places within us, a very biblical thing. This woman, like too many others, had been sexually abused as a child over the course of many years. As they settled into prayer like I described in the previous chapters, she was able with the help of the Holy Spirit to "find" the young girl within her, who was of course scared and sad.

Jesus asked, "Where are you hiding?"

I'm in my bedroom, the young part said.

"May I come there with you?"

Please.

Jesus came, and there were tears; the mature woman was able to shed tears on behalf of her younger self. After a time, Jesus asked the little girl, "Where would you like to go?"

I want to leave this place, the young part said.[i]

So they left the house. My friends thought Jesus would then take her to a safe haven, which he nearly always does. But he stopped, and the two of them—this sweet little girl and Jesus—stood there in the yard, looking back at the house where the years of abuse took place.

"What would you like to do?" he asked.

I want to burn it down.

Which is a sweet and fiery thing for a little girl to say! But so warranted; it *needed* burning down.

Jesus then burnt the house to the ground. Then the two of

---

i.   Young parts fragmented through trauma are often stuck in the place the trauma happened. Jesus always wants to get them unstuck and out of that place.

them walked away, and a deep, lasting resolution happened for that woman that day.

Kingdom Visits

Saint Paul had a number of mystical experiences we know about. His encounter with Jesus on the Damascus Road would certainly be the most well known, as it should be. You can read that wild story in its fullness in Acts chapter 9. It is amphibious living demonstrated—from hearing the voice of Jesus right down to actual "scales" that fall from Paul's eyes when some guy Paul doesn't even know comes in to pray for him!

Paul also "visited" heaven at least once, but not in the manner of "near-death experiences" reported in a number of popular books in the past few decades. Paul was not near death. He was simply "summoned" one day to the presence of God. In the passage that follows, Paul tells this story as if it's about someone else ("I know a man in Christ who . . ."), but scholars generally agree that the overall context of the passage indicates Paul was speaking of himself:

> I will go on to visions and revelations from the Lord. I know a man in Christ who fourteen years ago was caught up to the third heaven. Whether it was in the body or out of the body I do not know—God knows. And I know that this man—whether in the body or apart from the body I do not know, but God knows—was caught up to paradise and heard inexpressible things, things that no one is permitted to tell. (2 Corinthians 12:1–4)

Isaiah was also summoned to the throne room of God (Isaiah 6). A prophet mystic named Micaiah tells of his visits to the Council of the Lord in 2 Chronicles 18. (In fact, you weren't considered a true prophet in Israel unless you had been to the heavens and the Council of the Lord.[13])

And of course, we have the almost *Lord of the Rings*–like narrative account of Saint John's visits to the Kingdom of God in the book of Revelation. Twenty-two chapters encompass his visits, including encounters and conversations with angels.

But is any of this available to the ordinary mystic?

Listen carefully again to this passage quoted earlier from the book of Hebrews: "So let us come boldly to the throne of our gracious God. There we will receive his mercy, and we will find grace to help us when we need it most" (Hebrews 4:16 NLT).

The invitation is to every believer; that is clear. It is not stated in a poetic or figurative manner—it is given quite literally. Come to the throne of grace; come to your Father in heaven. Ordinary saints and mystics through the ages took it literally, knowing that the throne of God is an actual place. So here we have an invitation, given to anyone who would seize it, to enter into the presence of God in the heavens.

Here is another:

You have not come to a mountain that can be touched and that is burning with fire; to darkness, gloom and storm; to a trumpet blast or to such a voice speaking words that those who heard it begged that no further word be spoken to them, because they could not bear what was commanded: "If even an animal touches the mountain, it must be stoned to death." The sight was so terrifying that Moses said, "I am trembling with fear."

But you have come to Mount Zion, to the city of the living God, the heavenly Jerusalem. You have come to thousands upon thousands of angels in joyful assembly, to the church of the firstborn, whose names are written in heaven. You have come to God, the Judge of all, to the spirits of the righteous made perfect, to Jesus the mediator of a new covenant, and to the sprinkled blood that speaks a better word than the blood of Abel. (Hebrews 12:18–24)

Let me ask—as you read this passage, do you regard the things being described as *real*? That the City of God is a real place, right now, as real as Cairo and Seattle, existing somewhere in God's great kingdom? It is.

What most people have overlooked is the phrase "you have come."

This is directed to the reader of the passage, and it is making an assumption about reality and relationship—by the power of God and his Spirit, we are right now participants in the City of God. You, the reader, *have come* to the City of God. As Paul says, we are citizens of heaven right now (Philippians 3:20), an active, current amphibious reality. He also says that we are seated, right now, with Christ at the right hand of the Father (Ephesians 2:6). Which also puts us in the center of the City of God. Now. In this present moment.

You have come.

Yet few ever ask to see it. Bernard of Clairvaux did. With the humility and gentleness of a true mature mystic, he hints at visiting the City of God—or at least seeing it—in this account:

Oh Sion, thou city sole and single, mystic mansions hidden in the heavens, now I rejoice in thee, now I moan for thee and mourn thee. Thee I often pass through in the heart, as I cannot in the body, for being earthly flesh and fleshly earth, soon I fall back.[14]

"Fall back" implies he was lifted up to some place to fall back *from*, and he names that place as the City of God. I appreciate Bernard speaking of the vision or visit as facilitated in, through, and by the heart; that has certainly been true for me and the mystics I know.

I know several mystics who have "been" to the City as well, or seen it, or been given a vision of it. The mystic doesn't really care. Remember—if you allow for mystery, you can experience God in many ways. If you demand the latest scientific proof of it, like a faithful Internet Disciple, you won't enjoy much at all.[ii]

The River of Life

We saw in chapter 13 that the River of Life is an actual river; it flows not only in the Kingdom of God (in the City and out into the countryside) but also within our hearts, as Jesus promised in John 7:38. Psalm 1 and Jeremiah 17 speak of our lives as planted by that river, drawing supernatural resilience from it, and the River of Life has been a source of healing and nourishment for many saints.

"Come to the river" as an invitation has been a staple of gospel songs for centuries.[15] There are many current gospel songs with the same invitation:

---

ii. To show you the playfulness of Jesus and the daily delight of the mystic life, as I am writing this section on the City of God, two songs play on my Spotify list: "City of God" by Stephanie Gretzinger and "Dreaming of Eden" by Tenielle Nada. So sweet.

Come to the River
All who are thirsty
Come and drink.[16]

Certainly we can "come to the River" as we commune with Jesus in our hearts, for he is there in actual presence, and the River is there as he promised.

"All I can tell you is this," a man wrote to me. "I was in a place of profound anguish. Jesus invited me: 'Come to the River with me.' The next thing I knew, we were there. It was very beautiful, like a real river but very clear. He told me to get in, and as soon as I did I could feel Life itself washing over me, cleansing me, renewing me. It was one of the most refreshing experiences I've had in prayer, ever, and I have returned many times since."

The mystic doesn't need to understand the mechanics. Do these encounters take place in our innermost being only, or do some of them take place in the rest of God's great Kingdom as the Spirit of God enables? My answer to these questions is that it doesn't really matter; don't get lost in the how, recovering Disciple of the Internet.

During an exercise of prayer, a man and wife I know each had the same experience without speaking of it until afterward. (Jesus will often bring this kind of confirmation to assure us *it was real*.) Jesus invited them to see into the Kingdom of God, and they "found themselves" at the River of Life as it flows through the countryside beyond the City of God (just as Ezekiel saw). This couple had gone through a devastating miscarriage many years ago.

As they lingered with Jesus in what he was showing them, they both saw their miscarried son and knew immediately it was him. They got to embrace him and tell him they loved him. It healed a wound of grief that had lingered in their souls for decades.

After the time of prayer, the husband tentatively brought the encounter up. "Honey, I had a pretty incredible experience. I saw our son . . ."

She began to weep. "I saw the same exact thing."

You can't make this stuff up; the imagination doesn't work like that. This is the sort of thing God does. He has invited many ordinary mystics down through the ages to see and experience various parts of the rest of reality, his beautiful Kingdom.

These gifts can be utter consolation and also fortification to press on through the battle.

Above All, Intimacy

There is so much more to say, but you will find it for yourself as you practice these things. Jesus will lead you in *intercession for others*; He will sometimes give *revelations regarding the future*.

But we never chase those things. The treasure is Jesus himself, and our Papa, and the Holy Spirit.

A friend called the other day and told me, "I had the most beautiful time this morning through the Prayer of Descent. I was suddenly before the throne of God, our Father. It wasn't scary at all, nothing like I expected. He was so loving and kind. I felt prompted to run and jump in his lap, but I was shy to do so. I looked over, and Jesus nodded. *Go ahead.* So I ran and jumped in Papa's lap! I fit like a child, fully wrapped in his arms."

A few days later I spoke with a mystic friend I hadn't seen for years. She confessed to me, "That passage in Psalms—how 'One day in your courts is better than a thousand days elsewhere'? I never liked that passage; I never understood it. But I have been drawn into an intimacy with Jesus that explains everything. I'm 'communing' with him in my heart every morning. Often I just start weeping, it is so beautiful."

We are highly relational beings made for intimacy with a highly relational Trinity—not just figuratively but in regular, nourishing experiences. These encounters strengthen our faith and deepen our union with Jesus. They change the way we move and operate in The World, situated securely in God.

Now, I must tell you—in terms of spiritual opposition and the anger of the enemy, this was the most difficult chapter of the book for me to write. It will be the one most hotly questioned when the book is published. Saint John of the Cross will tell you why: "The devil fears a soul in union with God as he fears God himself."

> **WE ARE HIGHLY RELATIONAL BEINGS MADE FOR INTIMACY WITH A HIGHLY RELATIONAL TRINITY—NOT JUST FIGURATIVELY BUT IN REGULAR, NOURISHING EXPERIENCES.**

The first time I read that, I was stunned. It made so much sense of the warfare the friends of Jesus experience. The devil fears a soul in union with God as he fears God himself. Satan is perfectly happy to let the Church talk about God, teach about God, scold in the name of God. What he fears are men and women actually coming to God, cultivating deep intimacy and union with Christ.

The Lord Jesus is making these experiences I've named, and many more, widely available to his people, for we are hard-pressed in this hour and we deeply need them. And remember, these things happen "not because He loved and attended to them more than He does to us, but because they loved and attended to Him more than we do."[17]

Let that fuel your heart and soul to press in all the more.

PAUSE

Breathe.

What are you thinking?

Is there something you would like to ask Jesus?

18.

Only You, and What You're Doing

All consolation that does not come from God is but desolation;
when the soul has learned to receive no comfort but in
God only, it has passed beyond the reach of desolation.

PERE LACOMBE

We have covered many things in these pages.

We set out recognizing that as Disciples of the Internet, our souls have been conditioned to expect immediate answers to our questions and to distrust all forms of mystery; we've developed an addiction to knowledge and the "practical" as the real stuff of life, even while the constant erosion of facts has undermined our ability to trust and believe.

I pray your soul is being healed from some of that now.

For we are amphibious creatures, designed by our Father not only to move comfortably between the seen and unseen, the material and the spiritual, but to *derive our well-being* through the nourishment that both parts of God's Kingdom provide. Postmodern life has cut most people off from half of the environment they were designed for, and we are dying in the lack of it.

We looked to the mystics for guidance on how to get out of this terrible mind-set and back into the fullness of life in God. Refuge is a primary and urgent need, and so we focused on refuge as the point at which we would reenter God's provision for us.

What Remains to Be Said?

At this point, more words and teaching feel unkind, maybe even indulgent. Let's not keep pouring wine into a glass that is already quite full.

How best to bring this conversation to rest?

Allow me some fatherly counsel, as if you had come to my hermitage in the woods. There is so much I want to say, but I will limit myself to one idea, one piece of advice explored from several angles, so that it stands out to you with clarity.

The Fundamental Problem

Keep choosing God.

Then choose him again.

And then again.

This is your task, your daily calling, whatever else you might be up to. Everything around you is pulling against it like a riptide.

I wish that One Great Choosing on our part would take care of things for the rest of our lives, but it doesn't work that way. You live in a story, not a painting. Things are very dynamic, as we saw in Psalm 91; you have to keep choosing, and choosing, and choosing Jesus *above all things*. This is how we love him and take refuge in him.

Keep me safe, my God,
for in you I take refuge.
I say to the LORD, "You are my Lord;
apart from you I have no good thing." (Psalm 16:1–2)

In other words, "you are my everything." The ordinary mystic has tasted enough of the goodness of God to need no convincing that this intimacy is worth anything it might cost.

What could possibly get in our way?

Prone to wander, Lord, I feel it,
prone to leave the God I love;
here's my heart; O take and seal it;
seal it for thy courts above.[1]

We are not yet wholehearted; parts of us are still double-minded. This reality has brought anguish and near despair to saints, mystics, and Jesus-friends down through the centuries. Why can't we stay in that one sweet place of union with Christ?

Our essential problem is this: We want two things that are in fundamental conflict with one another:

We truly do want Jesus. We do.

We *also* want a good life; it pulls on us every moment.

There are seasons when those things seem to be compatible. Until they are not. Like our dear brothers and sisters in parts of the world where they face fierce persecution and martyrdom at the hands of Islamist jihadist groups or oppressive governmental regimes. But in the developed world, where we have the entire base of human knowledge available to us in a few clicks *and* same-day delivery, the conflict is far less clear to us. The Church in the West has assured folks that they can live two lives: "You can have Jesus, *and* you can have a wonderful life! In fact, this is God's will for you!"

It is not true.

Of course your Father is a good Papa, and he *loves* to bless his children. Absolutely.

But there comes a time in your life with him that you will have to choose God over everything else . . . for the rest of your life.

Every saint, mystic, and friend of Jesus through the ages will tell you so. Jesus has told you so many times in the Gospels. We have parables like the ten bridesmaids, the sower and the seed, the man who wanted to store up wealth in bigger barns. We have blunt statements by Jesus like this one: "No one who puts a hand to the plow and looks back is fit for service in the kingdom of God" (Luke 9:62).

> THERE COMES A TIME IN YOUR LIFE WITH HIM THAT YOU WILL HAVE TO CHOOSE GOD OVER EVERYTHING ELSE . . . FOR THE REST OF YOUR LIFE.

I just looked up that verse online (there's the Internet life we all take for granted), and as I was reading, little ads perfectly targeted to my shopping habits kept flashing at me. How much more blatant of an example do we want? I'm on a Bible website for heaven's sake, and still the message sneaks in: *Sure, you can have Jesus. And, you can also have all these little niceties that make you feel better!*

"Watch and pray so that you will not fall into temptation. The spirit is willing, but the flesh is weak" (Matthew 26:41). Jesus said that too.

You Must Surrender the Self-Life Daily

Blaise Pascal became a Christian late in life, perhaps in great part due to the prayers of his sister. His first encounter with Jesus was deeply mystical; he never wrote about it publicly, but he scribbled out passionate notes during the encounter containing these phrases:

> FIRE.
>
> GOD of Abraham, GOD of Isaac, GOD of Jacob
> not of the philosophers and of the learned.
> Certitude. Certitude. Feeling. Joy. Peace.
> GOD of Jesus Christ.
> My God and your God.
> Your GOD will be my God.
> Forgetfulness of the world and of everything except GOD.
> He is only found by the ways taught in the Gospel.
> Grandeur of the human soul.
> Righteous Father, the world has not known you, but I
> have known you.
> Joy, joy, joy, tears of joy.[2]

When Pascal died, his servant found a piece of parchment containing these words sewn into the lining of his jacket. He kept them close to his heart after that remarkable encounter with Jesus on the night of his salvation.

That account is fairly well known. What is less well known is that Pascal, a passionate gambler, lived a very austere life after his conversion:

> According to Gilberte (his sister) . . . he championed the ideal of
> poverty and claimed that one should prefer and use goods crafted

by the poorest and most honest artisans, not those manufactured by the best and most accomplished. He purged his home of luxuries and pretty furnishings and took in a homeless family.[3]

It was Pascal's way of dealing with the fundamental conflict every soul faces: desiring Christ while at the same time chasing "the good life." If you read the mystics, nearly every single one of them talks about how to "mortify the flesh" due to the heartbreak they felt upon discovering how easily they could turn from the One they loved, not in apostasy but simply in the indulgence of what I call the Self-Life.

The Self-Life is that part of you that wants its way, like a toddler. It wants life to be easy; it wants to be seen and praised; it wants to be the focus of your attention. It is easily offended, and it resents (and hates) anyone or anything that gets in its way. The Self-Life is irritated when church services run long, and it balked at what I suggested for morning and evening prayer; in fact, it has given you many reasons not to pray over the years. The Self-Life is committed to the good life.

The Self-Life is going to undermine your best efforts to stay in the refuge of God; you must surrender it to Jesus daily—sometimes many times a day. "Jesus, I give you the Self-Life, and all Selfhood." This gets me out of myself and back to him.

Practice choosing against your will (especially your indulgences) to weaken the Self-Life's grip on you. As Brother Lawrence affirmed,

Do not be discouraged by the resistance you will encounter from your human nature; you must go against your human inclinations. Often, in the beginning, you will think that you are wasting

231

time, but you must go on, be determined and persevere in it until death, despite all the difficulties.[4]

This is critical for those living in the unprecedented comfort culture of the Western world, where relief is instantly accessible in so many ways.

The Sin of Esau

Scripture contains many warnings not to give in, give up, or let our hearts be taken captive by anything other than Christ. I think of Jesus urging us to "remember Lot's wife!" which is a very sober warning indeed (Luke 17:32), and his parable of the ten bridesmaids (Matthew 25). But a less-known warning, tucked into the text toward the end of the book of Hebrews, feels terribly relevant to the situation I've been describing above:

See that no one is . . . godless like Esau, who for a single meal sold his inheritance rights as the oldest son. Afterward, as you know, when he wanted to inherit this blessing, he was rejected. Even though he sought the blessing with tears, he could not change what he had done. (Hebrews 12:16–17)

Esau was the eldest son of Isaac and in line to be the heir of God's promise to Abraham's descendants. He was "a skillful hunter, a man of the open country" (Genesis 25:27). The story goes that Esau returned one day from hunting empty-handed, utterly dejected, and delirious with hunger. Who knows how long he was out there in the wild, but the man was in bad shape. Jacob was enjoying dinner, and Esau begged him for some:

Once when Jacob was cooking some stew, Esau came in from the open country, famished. He said to Jacob, "Quick, let me have some of that red stew! I'm famished!" . . .

Jacob replied, "First sell me your birthright."

"Look, I am about to die," Esau said. "What good is the birthright to me?"

But Jacob said, "Swear to me first." So he swore an oath to him, selling his birthright to Jacob.

Then Jacob gave Esau some bread and some lentil stew. He ate and drank, and then got up and left.

So Esau despised his birthright. (Genesis 25:29–34)

This is a troubling story. What is the meaning? Why are we warned of repeating this catastrophic failure?

The sin of Esau at its core is *choosing relief over God*. You know this precipice very well. When you are tired and worn out, you just want relief. When you are beat up by this world and losing heart, you just want relief. When you are traumatized, you just want relief.

And when you live in the world of instant answers and same-day delivery, relief is pretty darn easy to come by. Be brutally honest as you let yourself give a gut response to this question: Which feels more reliable to you; which gives you more *immediate* relief: God or your cell phone? When you're bored, waiting in line for carpool or for a delayed flight, which do you instinctively reach for?

Turn Your Back on The World

Let's return for a moment to the scene in the Judean wilderness where Satan was circling Jesus' camp like a cunning predator, calculating an opportunity to take him down. Jesus was in the same condition as Esau if not worse—he was weary from forty days of living outside, sleeping on the ground, exposed to the elements, fasting. Satan tried to end God's redemptive plan simply by offering Jesus . . . relief.

Jesus refused it.

So must we.

There comes a point in every maturing mystic's life where we must decide to turn our back on The World and all of its indulgences, distractions, intrigues, corruption, and blasphemies. Instead, we seek relief (consolation, succor) though intimacy with God and experiences of his Kingdom. It's not that we don't seek relief; it's *where* we seek it. Daily, the maturing mystic draws upon all that Christ is giving for relief and restoration. The provision is always there!

Folks, The World is a shipwreck from which every man, woman, and child must swim for their life. We each face this choice in very particular ways. Jesus might ask you not to attend the annual family reunion, and suddenly your allegiances are exposed. He might ask you to pass up the PhD, and your identity is suddenly shaken to the core. He might ask you to give away more of your income than you planned, and your security is threatened in ways you didn't think it would be.

If you do not choose to turn your back on The World, you will find your intimacy with Jesus slipping away. And if you think I'm overstating this, just notice the cycle of weariness and relief in your own life over the next few weeks. It's sobering; it's far too close to the sin of Esau.

The Only Safe Place

We set out in search of refuge. Let us come back around to it once more.

Standing between a ship and the dock, the most dangerous

thing to do is to linger with one foot on the dock and one in the boat. This is where most accidents take place. The same holds true of any subway or train.

Friends, there is only one safe place in the cosmos: to be situated deeply in Jesus Christ. There is no other. You can't have one foot in and the other out. You must choose to be all-in, every remaining day of your life. Most of the time, this will be an absolute joy. But there are times it will require a sheer act of will, and other times it will be very costly.

Honestly, I feel like I'm trying to persuade a pod of whales to come back to the sea. *Please stay in the ocean; please. It's the only safe place for you.* God is the ocean, the habitat we were made for; he is our one and only home. As C. S. Lewis confessed,

> This is my endlessly recurrent temptation: to go down to that Sea (I think St. John of the Cross called God a sea) and there neither dive nor swim nor float, but only dabble and splash, careful not to get out of my depth and holding on to the lifeline which connects me with my things temporal.
>
> Swimming lessons are better than a lifeline to the shore. For of course that lifeline is really a death line.[5]

It sure is.

The practices I've presented in this book are swimming lessons for mystics. If indeed you *do* practice them, swimming in the ocean of God will become second nature. But then, those who have tasted the presence of God know that there is no other place they *want* to be. The best "mortification" of the Self-Life and its love affair with The World is the incomparable bliss we have in Papa, Jesus, Holy Spirit, and the wonders of the Kingdom.

THOSE WHO HAVE TASTED THE PRESENCE OF GOD KNOW THAT THERE IS NO OTHER PLACE THEY *WANT* TO BE.

So choose God.

Then choose him again.

And then again.

This is your daily task for the rest of your life.

Often, when I return to God in prayer or simply give him my attention throughout the day, I will say, *There you are, my Bliss.*

Those who live in the shelter of the Most High
> will find rest in the shadow of the Almighty.

This I declare about the LORD:

He alone is my refuge, my place of safety;
> he is my God, and I trust him.

For he will rescue you from every trap
> and protect you from deadly disease.

He will cover you with his feathers.
> He will shelter you with his wings.
> His faithful promises are your armor and
> > protection.

Do not be afraid of the terrors of the night,
> nor the arrow that flies in the day.

Do not dread the disease that stalks in darkness,
> nor the disaster that strikes at midday.

Though a thousand fall at your side,
> though ten thousand are dying around you,
> these evils will not touch you.

Just open your eyes,
>   and see how the wicked are punished.
If you make the Lord your refuge,
>   if you make the Most High your shelter,
no evil will conquer you;
>   no plague will come near your home.
For he will order his angels
>   to protect you wherever you go.
They will hold you up with their hands
>   so you won't even hurt your foot on a stone.
You will trample upon lions and cobras;
>   you will crush fierce lions and serpents under
>   your feet!
The Lord says, "I will rescue those who love me.
>   I will protect those who trust in my name.
When they call on me, I will answer;
>   I will be with them in trouble.
>   I will rescue and honor them.
I will reward them with a long life
>   and give them my salvation. (NLT)

APPENDIX 1

The Prayer of Descent

Finding Jesus Within You

AN EXCERPT FROM *RESILIENT*[1]

First, let's name the "levels" of our being:

- You have fleeting thoughts throughout the day, most of which are insignificant.
- You also have longings, hopes, and dreams that are far more important.
- Deep within you, you have experienced the cry for love, hope, and joy, which feels almost primal to your being.

I call these layers of our being the Shallows, Midlands, and Depths.

The Shallows of our being are characterized and ruled by the distractions of life. In the shallows we flit from thought to thought, distraction to distraction almost unpredictably.

The Midlands are characterized and ruled by what I, echoing Jesus' words, would call "the cares of life," the deeper worries, heartaches, longings, and aspirations that occupy the human heart (see Luke 21:34 and Matthew 4:19). When Jesus said, "Watch yourselves, lest your hearts be weighed down with . . . the cares of this life" (Luke 21:34 ESV), this is the geography of heartache and fear he is referring to.

Distractions keep you in the Shallows for much of your day. They burn mental energy and take your focus on a roller coaster ride. But it is the pressures of the Midlands that keep you up at night—those are the things that cause us to pray, the things that give us ulcers. The Midlands, not the Shallows, tend to be the place of our tears.

Deeper still, down in the "depths of your being," is the essence of your existence, and the dwelling place of God (now that you have invited him to live in you!). The Depths are characterized and ruled by eternal things like faith, hope, love, and joy, to name a few.

We all have a deep inner life, whether we pay attention to it or not. This is very hopeful, because we *can* learn to access it.

How Do We Descend?

We are looking to find the presence of God in our inmost being, to experience him and commune with him there. By tapping into his actual presence within us, we are able to receive the strength that prevails. It begins with simply giving him your attention.

We set aside a time to give God our undivided attention (the battle is always for your attention). The new thought is that we are giving our attention to God-who-lives-within-us. As we tune out the world around us and tune in to our hearts, we become aware of some form of the presence of Jesus-within-us.

Finding God always begins with loving him.

Just begin to love Jesus, or your Father, or the Holy Spirit within you. *I love you, God. I love you, God. I love you.* Settle in, knowing you are taking it slowly. *I love you, God. I love you, God. I love you.* As we do this, we intentionally leave the distractions of the Shallows. We tune them out; we choose to ignore them. We begin to drop into our own being. As we consciously and intentionally love Jesus-within-us, it allows his Spirit to guide us into communion with him.

Try It

Find a quiet place. In a busy home even the bathroom or a closet will work because you can shut the door. Do not bring your phone. If you need it for a timer or for music, put it on airplane mode. Get your body into a comfortable position, like pulling your knees up to your chest and wrapping your arms around your knees. I don't recommend lying down because you'll fall asleep (we are all so weary). Sometimes a comfy blanket can assist you in "settling in."

I will play soft, instrumental music in the background on occasion, but *only* as a backdrop to create a sacred space, not as something asking for my attention. No lyrics—only gentle, quiet instrumental music.[i]

Start with a simple prayer:

Jesus—I long for your presence, Lord. Help me commune with you where you live inside of me.

---

i. "Soaking in His Presence" by William Augusto is a favorite of ours for this purpose. "Soaking in His Presence," YouTube channel, accessed July 2, 2024, https://www.you tube.com/c/SoakinginHisPresence.

Repeat that several times over. Repetition is really helpful in this kind of prayer. I'll repeat things over and over as I tune in.

As you quiet yourself, practice some benevolent detachment:

> *Jesus, I give everyone and everything to you, God.*
> *I give everyone and everything to you.*

Repeat that a few times. If something keeps trying to distract you, specifically give the issue over to God:

> *I give you my children; my work; that email.*

But don't get caught up in a whole laundry-list of cares; just ignore the Shallows and keep tuning into Jesus-within-you. Ask the Holy Spirit for his help:

> *Holy Spirit, help me to descend.*
> *Help me locate Christ in me.*
> *Help me follow Christ down into the depths of my being.*
> *I pray to commune with you there.*

Begin loving Jesus, or your Father, or the Holy Spirit *within you* (not looking to the Lord above, nor to Christ by your side, but looking within).

> *I love you, God. I love you, God. I love you.*

Settle in, knowing you are taking it slowly.

> *I love you, God. I love you, God. I love you.*

Become aware of Jesus-within-you, and follow him deeper within. Be open to what he wants to do. It might be comfort, it might be a word from God, or he might want to show you something. Let him take the lead.

This is not a time for typical prayer. Don't start praying for the cares you hold up in the Midlands. Don't intercede for others. This precious time is dedicated to one thing only—communion with God. As you linger there, ask God for his glorious strength:

Father, Jesus, Holy Spirit, fill the depths of my being with your glory. Fill me with your glory, Lord. Fill me with the river of life in my inmost being. Let the river flow in me. Give me the strength that prevails, Lord. Fill me with your glorious strength. I pray for supernatural resilience.

APPENDIX 2

A More Robust Daily Prayer

As we mature in our life with Jesus and his Kingdom, as we grow comfortable operating in the reality of the heavens, and as we take our place ever more effectively in his service, the kingdom of darkness will ramp up its efforts against us. We'll also find that the world is a very corrupting place, and that broken people—however much we love them—still have the capacity to sin against us, curse us, or create unhealthy ties with us. Living with freedom from what Patrick called "every cruel merciless power that may oppose my body and soul" requires much more authoritative and specific prayer.

For one thing, many people forget that when we are dealing with foul spirits, we are dealing with ancient beings of great intelligence and malice. They don't always yield with a quick, general prayer. We often have to be specific and commanding.

This robust morning prayer is a reflection of what my ministry team and I have found necessary.[i]

---

i. We often amend the prayer as we go if we find that we need to sanctify some aspect of our personality more specifically to Christ, be firm with certain foul spirits by name, or keep the cross of Christ between us and certain toxic people. Let this be a sort of guide but not a binding formula.

My dear Lord Jesus, beautiful Jesus, I come to you now to be restored in you, to be renewed in you, in full and complete union. Full and complete union. I run to you now and take refuge in you.

I love you, Jesus. I love you, Lord. And I give myself to you now—my entire life, being, and creation.

I give you my spirit, soul, and body. My mind, thought, and all mental life—every level. My will and motive. My heart in all its dimensions, all its life. I give you my understanding, discernment, and perception, along with all prophetic gifting, all vision and hearing and Kingdom living. My sexuality and sensitivity, empathy, and conscience. Heart and soul, mind and strength, body temple, spirit. Everything.

I withhold nothing. And I bring the cleansing Blood of the Lord Jesus Christ throughout all. I cleanse my entire created being with the Blood of the Lord Jesus, and I ask your Holy Spirit to restore me in you, renew me in you, and lead this time of prayer. In all that I now pray I stand in absolute utter agreement with you, Lord Jesus, and with everyone who is praying for me by the Spirit in heaven and on earth.

Dearest God, holy and victorious Trinity, you alone are worthy of all of my love, my worship, my trust. I give myself to you in my heart's search for life. You alone are life, God, and you have become my life. I renounce the Self-Life this morning. I renounce Satan, his kingdom, and The World. And I give to you, God, the place in my heart, in my household, and in my kingdom that you truly deserve. I worship you.

I ask your forgiveness for my every sin. I renounce sin and all it has given the enemy in my life. Search me, know me, reveal to me where you are working in my life, and grant to me your healing, deliverance, holiness, and a deep true repentance.

Heavenly Father, thank you for loving me and choosing me before you made the world. I love you, Papa. I love you, God. I give myself to be as one with you, just as Jesus is one with you in all things. Papa, thank you for proving your love for all ages in Jesus Christ. Thank you for giving your Son to atone for my sins through his shed Blood. Thank you for re-creating me in Christ, for making me whole and complete in him. Thank you for raising me with him and reinstating me at your right hand. Thank you for anointing me, Father, with the fullness of your Glory, Love, and Kingdom. I receive it with thanks and I give it utter claim to my life.

I bring the life and work of the Lord Jesus in all its fullness over, around, through, and throughout our union—my spirit, soul, and body; my mind and thought; all my mental life, will, and motives; my understanding, discernment, and perception; all my prophetic vision and hearing and all kingdom living; my sexuality and sensitivity; heart and soul, mind and strength, body temple, and spirit. I bring the life and work of Jesus Christ throughout my home and household, my kingdom and domain.

Jesus, thank you for coming to ransom me, restore me, renew me, re-create me, and reinstate me. I love you, Lord. I love you, Jesus. I give everything for your everything. I pray for union; I pray for oneness. I receive again all the work and triumph in the cross, and I take my place in the cross immediately, dying with you to the Self-Life, to sin, to Satan and his forces, to the world and its corruptions, to the church in sin. I take up the cross and crucify the Self-Life now, with all pride, hatred, all hatred of you, all forms of murder and lust, all forms of fear and doubt and unbelief. I crucify the flesh, and I put off the old man.

I bring the Cross, Blood, and sacrifice of the Lord Jesus over, around, through, and throughout our union in every level of my being—throughout my spirit, soul, and body; my mind, thought, and all mental life; my will and motives; my heart in all dimensions; throughout my understanding, discernment, perception, and all prophetic gifting; my sexuality and sensitivity. Heart and soul, mind and strength, body temple, spirit. I bring the Cross, Blood, and sacrifice of the Lord Jesus Christ throughout my home, household, kingdom, and domain.

Jesus, I also sincerely receive you as my life. You are my life, and I give everything I am to your life in me. I am saved by your life. I reign in life through your life, and so I enter your life immediately. I enter your life, Jesus, and I receive your hope, joy, love, and faith; your glory, beauty, goodness, and trueness; your wisdom, cunning, and brilliance; your courage, power, and glory; holy love and holy life in everything.

I bring the life, the resurrection, and the River of Life through and throughout our union in every level of my being—throughout my spirit, soul, and body; my mind, thought, and all mental life; my will and motives; my heart in all dimensions, throughout my understanding, discernment, perception, and all prophetic gifting; my sexuality and sensitivity. Heart and soul, mind and strength, body temple, spirit. I bring the life, the resurrection, and the River of Life throughout my home, household, kingdom, and domain.

Jesus, I also sincerely receive all the work and triumph

*in your authority, in your ascension, and in your throne. All
authority in the heavens and on the earth is given to you,
Lord. Satan has been judged; his kingdom is overthrown.
And you, Lord Jesus, have been given the name above all
other names at which every knee bows. And so immediately
I take my place in your authority, ascension, and throne. I
ascend in my heart and I ascend in the heavens. Holy Spirit,
help me to ascend immediately.*

*Jesus, I bring all things of my kingdom and all things of
my domain under your rule and into your Kingdom again,
right now—this home, family, household, all goods and services, tools, equipment, vehicles, finances, this property, my
work in the world, all things of my kingdom and domain.
And I release and command the very fullness of your Glory,
Love, and Kingdom throughout my kingdom and domain.*

*Standing with you now, in you now, in the name of the
Lord Jesus Christ I command Fire, Glory, judgment, wrath
from the hand of the Lord God Almighty and from the Lord
Jesus Christ—the full sweep of heaven, judgment absolute
and final—on the forces of darkness that assailed me [or us]
in the night, and all that are arrayed against me [or us] in
this new day. Fire, Glory, judgment, wrath, the full sweep
of heaven upon every ruler, authority, power, and spiritual
force of wickedness of every kind, including their servants,
backups, weapons, and devices.[ii]*

*Fire, Glory, judgment, wrath from the hand of the Lord
God Almighty and from the Lord Jesus Christ cutting off and*

---

ii. It helps at this point to get specific and name what's been assaulting you or what you
know has been released in the world. Given what has been released by the kingdom of
darkness, I would include what I've listed in the prayer.

consuming all hatred, bitterness, and resentment—including all hatred, bitterness, and resentment of you, God.

The creation Glory and Breath of the Living God against all forms of chaos.

The River of Life, Breath, and Glory of the Lord God Almighty consuming all forms of death, destruction, and de-creation.

The Breath and Glory of the Lord Almighty and the Lord Jesus Christ against all antichrist spirits, powers, and devices; all hatred and death released against the saints; all desolation, desecration, and the apostasy. All of the Black Breath, fog, and poison. Every counterfeit God spirit, counterfeit Lord Jesus Christ, Father God, Holy Spirit.

Full, final, and immediate judgment upon all foul spirits, sparing only those that have permission to go immediately to the throne of the Lord Jesus Christ. This includes all of their servants, backups, forces, and every weapon, claim, and device. I release the heavenly host upon them now. Thank you, Lord God Almighty.

Jesus, I command the very fullness of your Body and Blood given in sacrifice, Fire, and Glory from the Lord God Almighty to destroy immediately all forms of foul powers, witchcraft, and black arts raised against me and my household. This includes all curses, rituals, and sacrifices, spells and veils, poisons and devices of every kind, destroyed immediately along with every empowering spirit.

I bring the Blood and Glory of the Lord Jesus Christ between me and The World at all times, between me and all of its corruptions. I filter all media coming into my home through the Blood of the Lord Jesus.

And finally, Lord Jesus, I command your Love and Kingdom, your Blood and Glory between me and every human being—their spirit, soul, and body; their sin, warfare, and all they are channeling for the enemy. I order every human spirit, altar, and fragment bound back to their own body with the cords of the Holy Spirit. I order their sin, warfare, corruption, contamination, and all they are channeling for the enemy cleansed and removed from me and my household with your Blood, Fire, and Glory. Only the love of the Lord Jesus between me and every human being.[iii]

I summon the heavenly host now in the name of the Lord Jesus Christ with love, honor, and blessing, and with love, honor, and blessing I ask them to carry out these orders to the uttermost and to help us in all things until all is done. Let the canopy around my home be rebuilt, cleansed, and sealed with your Blood and Glory. I ask for ministering angels to minister to us, your ministry.

Holy Spirit, thank you for coming. I love you. I worship you. I name you Lord absolute of everything I've named in my prayers and of all my kingdom and domain. Come, Holy Spirit—come and reign, come and rule in all things. I sanctify to you again today the fullness of my created being—heart and soul, mind and strength, body temple, spirit. Sanctify me through and through; restore my union with Jesus and with Papa. Anoint me, Holy Spirit, for the day, the week, and the hour. Fill all my relationships—family, friendships, neighbors, and strangers that I interact with.

Finally, Lord Jesus, I do put on the full combat gear of

---

iii. You probably want to name specific individuals at this point, such as clients, neighbors who rage at you, codependent family members, etc.

war, the full armor of God, and with you I command the very fullness of your Glory, Love, and Kingdom released throughout my kingdom and domain, filling all gaps now, filling all cleared-out spaces, finishing every command. In the name and in the authority of the Lord Jesus Christ of Nazareth, who came in the flesh, the only Jesus I ever name.

All glory to your name, Lord. Amen.

APPENDIX 3

A More Robust Bedtime Prayer

My dear Lord Jesus, I come to you now to be restored in you, take refuge in you, and be one with you in everything. As I come into your presence, I pause to give everyone and everything to you, God. Everyone. Everything. I give you my family and all people in my life.

I give you my work. I give you the day, the week, and I give you the future, Lord. I release all things in order to come back to you in full union and alignment.[i]

I consecrate to you again all of my created being—heart and soul, mind and strength, body temple, spirit. All of my emotions, all of my thoughts. And I bring the cleansing Blood of the Lord Jesus over, around, through, and throughout my heart and soul, mind and strength, body temple, and spirit. I cleanse our union with your Blood, Lord. Holy Spirit— restore me, renew me, and lead this time of prayer. In all

---

i. Linger here, releasing everything you know is burdening you. Be specific. Take your time.

that I now pray I stand in utter agreement with you, Jesus, and with everyone praying for me in heaven and on earth.

And now I ascend to you, Lord. Holy Spirit, help me to ascend. I ascend in my heart and I ascend in the heavens. In the name of the Lord Jesus Christ, I bring all things of this home and household, my kingdom and domain, under your rule and into your Kingdom.

Once again I call down Fire, Glory, judgment absolute and final upon the forces of darkness that have been arrayed against me [or us] this day, and all that are arrayed against me [or us] in this night to come. Fire, Glory, judgment absolute and final, sparing only those with permission to go immediately to the throne of the Lord Jesus Christ. Every ruler, authority, power, spiritual force of wickedness of every kind.[ii]

The Breath and Glory of the Lord Almighty and the Lord Jesus Christ against all antichrist spirits, powers, and devices; all hatred and death released against the saints; all desolation, desecration, and the apostasy. All of the Black Breath, fog, and poison.

Full, final, and immediate judgment upon all foul spirits, sparing only those that have permission to go immediately to the throne of the Lord Jesus Christ. This includes all of their servants, backups, forces, every weapon, claim, and device. I release the heavenly host upon them now. Thank you, Lord God Almighty.

Jesus, I command the very fullness of your body and

---

ii. At this point it helps to specifically name those evils that have been attacking you, such as chaos, hatred, or death. But because of the hour we live in, I would always include the ones in this prayer.

Blood given in sacrifice, with Fire and Glory from the Lord God Almighty to immediately destroy all forms of foul powers, witchcraft, and black arts raised against me and my household. This includes all curses, rituals and sacrifices, spells and veils, poisons and devices of every kind, destroyed immediately along with every empowering spirit.

I bring the Blood and Glory of the Lord Jesus Christ between me and The World at all times, between me and all of its corruptions. I filter all media coming into my home through the Blood of the Lord Jesus.

And finally, Lord Jesus, I command your Love and Kingdom, your Blood and Glory between me and every human being—their spirit, soul, and body, and their sin, warfare, and all they are channeling for the enemy. I order every human spirit, altar, and fragment bound back to their own body with the cords of the Holy Spirit. I order their sin, warfare, corruption, contamination, and all they are channeling for the enemy cleansed and removed from me and my household with your Blood, Fire, and Glory. Only the love of the Lord Jesus between me and every human being.

I summon the heavenly host once again, in the name of the Lord Jesus Christ, with love, honor, and blessing, and with love, honor, and blessing I ask them to carry out these orders to the uttermost and to help us in all things, until all is done. Let the canopy around my home be rebuilt, cleansed, and sealed with your Blood and Glory. I ask for ministering angels to minister to us, your ministry.

Holy Spirit, fill our home and our sleep tonight. I command all of this in the name of the Lord Jesus Christ, all glory to his name.

APPENDIX 4

Who I Am in Christ

BY NEIL ANDERSON[i]

I Am Accepted . . .

- I am God's child. (John 1:12)
- As a disciple, I am a friend of Jesus Christ. (John 15:15)
- I have been justified (declared righteous). (Romans 5:1)
- I am united with the Lord, and I am one with him in spirit. (1 Corinthians 6:17)
- I have been bought with a price and I belong to God. (1 Corinthians 6:19–20)
- I am a member of Christ's body. (1 Corinthians 12:27)
- I have been chosen by God and adopted as his child. (Ephesians 1:3–8)
- I have been redeemed and forgiven of all my sins. (Colossians 1:13–14)
- I am complete in Christ. (Colossians 2:9–10)

---

i. Taken from Neil T. Anderson, *Victory Over the Darkness: Realize the Power of Your Identity in Christ* (Gospel Light, 2000), 38–39, 53.

- I have direct access to the throne of grace through Jesus Christ. (Hebrews 4:14–16)

I Am Secure . . .

- I am free from condemnation. (Romans 8:1–2)
- I am assured that God works for my good in all circumstances. (Romans 8:28)
- I am free from any condemnation brought against me, and I cannot be separated from the love of God. (Romans 8:31–39)
- I have been established, anointed, and sealed by God. (2 Corinthians 1:21–22)
- I am hidden with Christ in God. (Colossians 3:1–4)
- I am confident that God will complete the good work he started in me. (Philippians 1:6)
- I am a citizen of heaven. (Philippians 3:20)
- I have not been given a spirit of fear but of power, love, and a sound mind. (2 Timothy 1:10)
- I am born of God and the evil one cannot touch me. (1 John 5:18)

I Am Significant . . .

- I am a branch of Jesus Christ, the true vine, and a channel of his life. (John 15:5)
- I have been chosen and appointed to bear fruit. (John 15:16)
- I am God's temple. (1 Corinthians 3:16)
- I am a minister of reconciliation for God. (2 Corinthians 5:17–21)

- I am seated with Jesus Christ in the heavenly realm. (Ephesians 2:6)
- I am God's workmanship. (Ephesians 2:10)
- I may approach God with freedom and confidence. (Ephesians 3:12)
- I can do all things through Christ, who strengthens me. (Philippians 4:13)

Acknowledgments

I have learned so much from so many people that I could not begin to do them justice here. My son Blaine Eldredge provided invaluable research assistance with this book; thank you, Blaine! My editor Daniel Marrs was, as always, wise, kind, and perceptive. This is a much better book because of him and my brilliant copyeditor, Natalie Nyquist. My sincere thanks also to the full team at Nelson Books, at Yates and Yates, and at Wild at Heart.

Notes

CHAPTER 1: HELP MY UNBELIEF!

1. Stephen Fein, "Effects of Suspicion on Attributional Thinking and the Correspondence Bias," *Journal of Personality and Social Psychology* 70, no. 6 (1996): 1164–84, https://doi.org/10.1037/0022-3514.70.6.1164.

2. Brother Lawrence, *The Practice of the Presence of God* (Spire Books, 1967), 44.

3. G. K. Chesteron, *Orthodoxy* (Bodley Head, 1908), 34.

4. J. Dudley Woodberry, "To the Muslim I Became a Muslim?," *International Journal of Frontier Missiology* 24, no. 1 (2007): 25, https://www.ijfm.org/PDFs_IJFM/24_1_PDFs/Woodberry.pdf.

CHAPTER 2: WHAT CHILDREN AND MYSTICS KNOW

1. As quoted in Thomas Cahill's *How the Irish Saved Civilization: The Untold Story of Ireland's Heroic Role from the Fall of Rome to the Rise of Medieval Europe* (Anchor Books, 1995), 117, who cites Kuno Meyer, trans., *Selections from Ancient Irish Poetry* (Constable, 1911), 26, archived at Project Gutenberg, last updated January 6, 2021, https://www.gutenberg.org/cache/epub/32030/pg32030-images.html.

2. Saint Francis, "The Canticle of the Sun," Franciscan Friars, accessed July 10, 2024, https://franciscanfriarscresson.org/the-canticle-of-the-sun/.

3. Henry van Dyke, "Joyful, Joyful, We Adore Thee" (1911), Hymnary,

accessed July 23, 2024, https://hymnary.org/text/joyful_joyful_we
_adore_thee.

4. Evelyn Underhill, *Mysticism: A Study in the Nature and Development
of Spiritual Consciousness* (Methuen, 1919), https://www.google.com
/books/edition/Mysticism/MZ-6Z5CnaLcC.

5. Hebrews 4:16 NKJV.

6. Thomas à Kempis, *The Imitation of Christ* (ADF Randolf, 1895), 67.

CHAPTER 3: GIMME SHELTER

1. William G. Dever, *Who Were the Early Israelites and Where Did
They Come From?* (Eerdmans, 2003), 35.

2. "Refugee Data Finder," UNHCR, accessed July 2, 2024, https://
www.unhcr.org/refugee-statistics/; "World Migration Report 2024,"
International Organization for Migration, accessed July 2, 2024,
https://worldmigrationreport.iom.int/msite/wmr-2024-interactive/.

3. Also, in 2023 the US had a record twenty-eight "billion-dollar
disasters." This beat the previous record of twenty-two from 2020.
Aiden Gardiner, "Disasters Forced 2.5 Million Americans from
Their Homes Last Year," *The New York Times*, February 22, 2024,
https://www.nytimes.com/2024/02/22/climate/climate-disasters
-survivors-displacement.html; John Bateman, "U.S. Struck with
Historic Number of Billion-Dollar Disasters in 2023," NOAA,
January 9, 2024, https://www.noaa.gov/news/us-struck-with-historic
-number-of-billion-dollar-disasters-in-2023.

4. Apsley Cherry-Garcia, *The Worst Journey in the World: Antarctic
1910–1913*, vol. 1 (Constable, 1922), 280, https://www.google.com
/books/edition/The_Worst_Journey_in_the_World_Antarctic/.

5. Cherry-Garcia, *Worst Journey*, 277.

6. Cherry-Garcia, 278–79.

7. Quoted in Susan C. Margolin, "Why Kids Love Building Forts—and
Why Experts Say They Might Need Them More Than Ever," *The
Washington Post*, May 18, 2020, https://www.washingtonpost.com
/lifestyle/2020/05/18/why-kids-love-building-forts-why-experts-say
-they-might-need-them-more-than-ever/.

8. Jeanne Guyon, *Experiencing God Through Prayer* (Whitaker House, 1984), 15.

CHAPTER 4: THE REFUGE OF GOD

1. Exodus 33:11 NKJV.
2. William Wordsworth, "Ode on Intimations of Immortality from Recollections of Early Childhood," archived at Poets.org, accessed July 10, 2024, https://poets.org/poem/ode-intimations-immortality -recollections-early-childhood.
3. Verses quoted this time from the New Living Translation.
4. A. W. Tozer, *The Pursuit of God* (Christian Publications, 1993), 13.

CHAPTER 5: THE TURNING OF THE HEART

1. Starlette Thomas, "New Book Introduces Readers to Harriet Tubman, the Public Mystic," Good Faith Media, April 10, 2023, https://goodfaithmedia.org/new-book-introduces-readers-to-harriet -tubman-the-public-mystic/.
2. Lawrence, *Practice of the Presence of God*, 45.
3. Robert Barron, *Thomas Aquinas: Spiritual Master* (Word on Fire Academic, 2022), 19.

CHAPTER 6: THE MYTH OF NEUTRALITY VERSUS THE CONSECRATED LIFE

1. Preston Sprinkle, *Embodied: Transgender Identities, the Church, and What the Bible Has to Say* (David C. Cook, 2021), 162.
2. Quoted in Nicholas Carr, "Meanings of the Metaverse: The Andreessen Solution," Rough Type, November 8, 2021, https://www .roughtype.com/?p=9020.
3. C. S. Lewis, *Christian Reflections*, ed. Walter Hooper (William B. Eerdmans, 1967), 33.

CHAPTER 7: TAKING REFUGE IN THE TRUTH

1. C. S. Lewis, *The World's Last Night and Other Essays* (1960; repr., HarperOne, 2017), 117.

2. Uri Hasson, "Time Regained: Using Storytelling to Share Memories Across Brains," iBiology, October 2019, MP4 video, 27:46, https://www.ibiology.org/neuroscience/storytelling-and-memories/.

3. James L. Nolan Jr., *The Therapeutic State: Justifying Government at Century's End* (New York University Press, 1998), 6.

4. C. H. Surgeon, *The Treasury of David*, vol. 4 (Marshall Brothers, 1881), 89.

5. Cahill, *How the Irish Saved Civilization*, 116–17.

6. C. S. Lewis, *George MacDonald: An Anthology* (1946; repr., HarperOne, 2001), 1.

7. Evagrius Ponticus, *Talking Back: A Monastic Handbook for Combating Demons* (Liturgical Press, 2009), 49.

CHAPTER 8: THE BREASTPLATE OF PATRICK

1. Brother Andrew, John Sherrill, and Elizabeth Sherrill, *God's Smuggler* (Signet Books, 1968), 100.

2. Cahill, *How the Irish Saved Civilization*, 116.

3. Cahill, 116–19.

4. Cahill, 116.

5. Cahill, 116–18.

6. C. S. Lewis, preface in Saint Athanasius, *On the Incarnation* (SPCK Publishing, 2011).

CHAPTER 9: LIONS, COBRAS, SCORPIONS

1. Matthias Henze, "God Shelters the Faithful: The Prayer of Psalm 91," TheTorah.com, 2020, https://www.thetorah.com/article/god-shelters-the-faithful-the-prayer-of-psalm-91.

2. Henze, "God Shelters the Faithful."

3. Craig A. Evans and H. Daniel Zacharias, eds., *Jewish and Christian Scripture as Artifact and Canon* (T&T Clark, 2009), 143.

4. Carl S. Ehrlich, "Balaam the Seer: From the Bible to the Deir 'Alla Inscription," TheTorah.com, 2018, https://www.thetorah.com/article/balaam-the-seer-from-the-bible-to-the-deir-alla-inscription.

CHAPTER 10: LOVE AS REFUGE

1. *TIME* Staff, "How Trolls Are Ruining the Internet," *TIME*, August 29, 2016, https://time.com/4457110/internet-trolls/.

CHAPTER 11: JESUS: THE INTEGRATING CENTER OF ALL THINGS

1. William Butler Yeats, "The Second Coming," in *The Collected Poems of W. B. Yeats* (Palgrave Macmillan, 1989), archived at Poetry Foundation, accessed July 11, 2024, https://www.poetryfoundation .org/poems/43290/the-second-coming.
2. "Peace (Shalom) Advent Word Study," BibleProject, November 30, 2017, https://bibleproject.com/explore/video/shalom-peace/.
3. Janini Fisher, *Healing the Fragmented Selves of Trauma Survivors: Overcoming Internal Self-Alienation* (Routlege, 2017), 4.
4. Athanasius, *On the Incarnation* (Saint Vladimir's Seminary Press, 2000), 26.
5. Leanne Payne, *The Healing Presence: Curing the Soul Through Union with Christ* (Baker Books, 1995).
6. George MacDonald, *Unspoken Sermons* (1906; repr., Johannesen, 2004), 456–57.
7. Thomas à Kempis, *The Imitation of Christ* (Bruce Publishing, 1940), 54, archived at Christian Classics Ethereal Library, accessed July 12, 2024, https://ccel.org/ccel/kempis/imitation/imitation.TWO.1.html.

CHAPTER 12: REINTEGRATION: THE HEALING OF FRAGMENTED PARTS

1. For the neuroscience of trauma fragmentation, see Ruth A. Lanius, Braeden A. Terpou, and Margaret C. McKinnon, "The Sense of Self in the Aftermath of Trauma: Lessons from the Default Mode Network in Posttraumatic Stress Disorder," *European Journal of Psychotraumatology* 11, no. 1 (2020), https://doi.org/10.1080/200081 98.2020.1807703.
2. Eugene Peterson, *A Long Obedience in the Same Direction: Discipleship in an Instant Society* (1980; repr., IVP, 2021).

CHAPTER 13: THE BLOOD AND THE RIVER

1. C. S. Lewis, *The Great Divorce* (1946; repr., HarperOne, 2002), 70–71.
2. Lewis, *Great Divorce*, 21.

CHAPTER 15: THE BREATH OF GOD

1. Robert Alter, *The Hebrew Bible: A Translation with Commentary* (W. W. Norton, 2018).
2. "Hawaiian Customs and Traditions," The Hawaiian Islands, accessed July 2, 2024, https://www.gohawaii.com/hawaiian-culture/traditions.
3. C. S. Lewis, *The Lion, the Witch and the Wardrobe* (1950; repr., HarperCollins, 1978), 168–69.
4. Jillian Mackenzie and Jeff Turrentine, "Air Pollution: Everything You Need to Know," NRDC, October 31, 2023, https://www.nrdc.org /stories/air-pollution-everything-you-need-know; "Delhi Smog: Schools and Colleges Shut as Pollution Worsens," BBC, November 17, 2021, https://www.bbc.com/news/world-asia-india-59258910; "How Air Pollution Is Destroying Our Health," World Health Organization, accessed July 2, 2024, https://www.who.int/news-room /spotlight/how-air-pollution-is-destroying-our-health.
5. J. R. R. Tolkien, *The Lord of the Rings* (1954; repr., HarperCollins, 1991), 847.
6. Tolkien, *Lord of the Rings*, 846.
7. Tolkien, 847–48.
8. Heinrich August Wilhelm Meyer, *Critical and Exegetical Handbook to the Epistle to the Ephesians and the Epistle to Philemon*, Critical and Exegetical Commentary on the New Testament (T&T Clark, 1884), s.v. "Ephesians 6:16"; Konstantin Nosov, *Ancient and Medieval Siege Weapons: A Fully Illustrated Guide to Siege Weapons and Tactics* (Lyons Press, 2005), 190–91.

CHAPTER 17: WHAT CAN I EXPECT?

1. Julian of Norwich, *Revelations of Divine Love*, ed. Grace Warrack (1373; repr., Methuen, 1901), 55–56. She goes on to say, "And in these words I saw a marvellous high mystery hid in God, which

mystery He shall openly make known to us in Heaven: in which knowing we shall verily see the cause why He suffered sin to come. In which sight we shall endlessly joy in our Lord God."

2. Brother Lawrence, "Fifth Letter," in *The Practice of the Presence of God* (1692; repr., Epworth Press, 1933), 15.

3. Saint Bonaventure, *The Life of Saint Francis* (J. M. Dent, 1904), 14.

4. Eddie L. Hyatt, *2000 Years of Charismatic Christianity* (Charisma House, 2002), 102.

5. Blaise Pascal, "Pascal's Memorial" (1654), archived at Christian Classics Ethereal Library, accessed July 16, 2024, https://www.ccel .org/ccel/pascal/memorial.i.html.

6. John Walsh, journal entry, February 24, 1751, quoted in Hyatt, *2000 Years of Charismatic Christianity*, 104.

7. Augustine, *Confessions*, trans. Albert C. Outler (Westminster John Knox Press, 1955), archived at Internet Medieval Sourcebook, Fordham University, accessed July 2, 2024, https://sourcebooks .fordham.edu/basis/confessions-bod.asp.

8. Quotation from volume 54 of Martin Luther, *Luther's Works*, ed. Theodore G. Tappert (Fortress Press, 1967), 21. Copyright © 1967 by Fortress Press. Used by permission. All rights reserved.

9. Carey Wallace, *Stories of the Saints: Bold and Inspiring Tales of Adventure, Grace, and Courage* (Workman, 2020), 191.

10. David Garrison, *A Wind in the House of Islam: How God Is Drawing Muslims Around the World to Faith in Jesus Christ* (WIGTake Resources, 2014), 239.

11. Jeanne Guyon, *Union with God* (Seedsowers, 1981), 1–2.

12. Teresa of Avila, *The Complete Works of Saint Teresa of Jesus*, trans. E. Allison Peers (Sheed & Ward, 1946), 65.

13. Michael S. Heiser, *The Unseen Realm: Recovering the Supernatural Worldview of the Bible* (Lexham, 2015), 239.

14. David Downing, *Into the Region of Awe: Mysticism in C. S. Lewis* (InterVarsity, 2005), 20.

15. One version comes from William Francis Allen, Charles Pickard Ware, and Lucy McKim Garrison, *Slave Songs of the United States*

(A. Simpson, 1867), https://library.si.edu/digital-library/book
/slavesongsofunit00alle.
16. "Come to the River" and "Housefires" from Allen, Ware, and
Garrison, *Slave Songs of the United States.*
17. Evelyn Underhill, *The Mystics of the Church* (Schocken, 1964),
12–13.

CHAPTER 18: ONLY YOU, AND WHAT YOU'RE DOING
1. From Robert Robinson, "Come Thou Fount of Every Blessing"
(1758), archived at Hymnary, accessed July 2, 2024, https://hymnary
.org/text/come_thou_fount_of_every_blessing.
2. Pascal, "Pascal's Memorial."
3. David Simpson, "Blaise Pascal," Internet Encyclopedia of Philosophy,
accessed June 20, 2024, https://iep.utm.edu/pascal-b/.
4. Lawrence, *Practice of the Presence of God.*
5. C. S. Lewis, *The Weight of Glory* (1941; repr., HarperOne, 2001), 187.

APPENDIX 1: THE PRAYER OF DESCENT
1. John Eldredge, *Resilient: Restoring Your Weary Soul in These
Turbulent Times* (Nelson Books, 2022), 138–52.

About the Author

John Eldredge is a bestselling author, a counselor, and a teacher. He is also affectionately known as "The Abbot" of Wild at Heart, a ministry devoted to helping people discover the heart of God, recover their own hearts in God's love, and learn to live in God's kingdom. John and his wife, Stasi, live near Colorado Springs, Colorado.

A spiritual father speaks to you weekly.

John's Weekly Video Update

Every Friday, John shares a brief video where he offers timely, personal thoughts about how to keep Jesus at the center of your life.

Sign up now at **WildAtHeart.org/Weekly**

A daily practice
for union with God.

The One Minute Pause App

Discover this life-giving guided experience—led by John Eldredge—to help you reconnect with God through a brief pause where you release everyone and everything to Him.

Now with new guided prayers and encounters based on *Experience Jesus. Really.*

Available now on the **Pause App.**

SCAN ME!

There is so much more.

WildAtHeart.org

Founded by John and Stasi Eldredge, Wild at Heart is a ministry devoted to helping men and women find healing, restoration, and identity in Christ. Explore resources like podcasts, events, and prayers for a deeper walk with God and community.

Learn more at **WildAtHeart.org**

SCAN ME!

Weekly conversations to fuel your soul.

Wild At Heart Podcast

Join us for the Wild at Heart weekly podcast—available in video and audio formats. Each week's conversation offers thoughts on how to love God and live free.

SCAN ME!

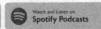

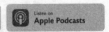

Don't do it alone.

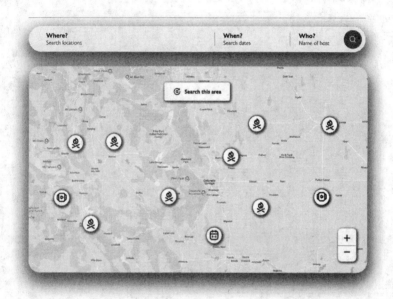

Wild At Heart Events

This journey with God is meant to be one experienced with others. There are thousands of Wild at Heart gatherings, events, and experiences happening all over the world...and near you!

Discover more at
WildAtHeart.org/Events

STORIES OF
BROKEN MEN
BECOMING REALLY
GOOD MEN.

GET YOUR HEART BACK.

The Wild At Heart Experience

Discover the path for recovering your masculine heart through this six-session video study.

Learn more at
WildAtHeart.org/WildAtHeart

SCAN ME!

The Captivating Experience

Explore the journey for restoring your feminine heart through this six-session video study.

Learn more at
WildAtHeart.org/Captivating

SCAN ME!

For your next small group study.

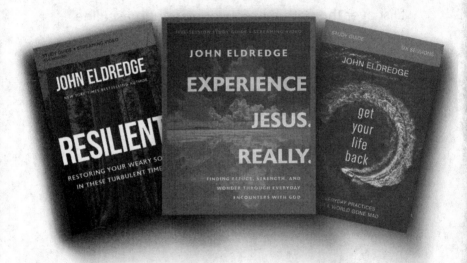

You can go deeper into the invitation of *Experience Jesus. Really.* through the video series and study guide. And if you already have, consider continuing the journey through *Get Your Life Back* and *Resilient* (the books as well as the accompanying video series and study guides). While each book is stand-alone, they also form a powerful trilogy of sorts when read together.

SCAN ME!

Learn more at **WildAtHeart.org/Books**